SCIENCE
FOUNDATIONS

Theory of Relativity

SCIENCE FOUNDATIONS

SCIENCE
FOUNDATIONS

Theory of Relativity

PHILLIP MANNING

CHELSEA HOUSE
An Infobase Learning Company

Science Foundations: Theory of Relativity
Copyright © 2012 by Infobase Learning

Chelsea House
An imprint of Infobase Learning
132 West 31st Street
New York, NY 10001

Library of Congress Cataloging-in-Publication Data
Manning, Phillip, 1936–
   Theory of relativity / Phillip Manning.
      p. cm. — (Science foundations)
   Includes bibliographical references and index.
   ISBN 978-1-60413-294-6 (hardcover)
   1. Relativity (Physics)—Juvenile literature. I. Title. II. Series.

   QC173.55.M365 2011
   530.11—dc22   2010047645

Chelsea House books are available at special discounts when purchased in bulk quantities for businesses, associations, institutions, or sales promotions. Please call our Special Sales Department in New York at (212) 967-8800 or (800) 322-8755.

You can find Chelsea House on the World Wide Web at
http://www.infobaselearning.com

Text design by Kerry Casey
Cover design by Alicia Post
Composition by EJB Publishing Services
Cover printed by Yurchak Printing, Landisville, Pa.
Book printed and bound by Yurchak Printing, Landisville, Pa.
Date printed: October 2011
Printed in the United States of America

10 9 8 7 6 5 4 3 2 1

This book is printed on acid-free paper.

All links and Web addresses were checked and verified to be correct at the time of publication. Because of the dynamic nature of the Web, some addresses and links may have changed since publication and may no longer be valid.

Contents

Relative Motion and the Laws of Physics

The theory of relativity was developed by theoretical physicist Albert Einstein early in the twentieth century. However, similar, if less complete, theories have been around much longer. One of the first scientists to investigate the idea of relativity was the seventeenth-century astronomer Galileo Galilei.

"Motion," he wrote in 1632, ". . . exists relatively to things that lack it; and among things which all share equally in any motion, it does not act, and is as if it did not exist." In other words, an object's motion exists only in relation to other objects. This concept was a big step toward our understanding of motion.

RELATIVE MOTION

No lengthy studies are needed to test Italian physicist Galileo Galilei's idea about the relativity of motion. Everyday experience confirms it. Consider an airplane with the shades pulled so that the passengers cannot see out. If the air is smooth, there is no way for them to know that they are zooming along at a steady 500 miles (805 kilometers) per hour relative to Earth. Within the cabin of the plane, it is, as Galileo says, as if the motion of the plane "did not exist."

Figure 1.1   Galileo Galilei, a physicist, mathematician, and philosopher, is often considered the father of modern science.

What happens to the laws of motion in that airplane? How would they compare to the laws determined by a physicist working in a lab on the Earth's surface? Galileo figured this out, too, but, of course, he could not use an airplane to illustrate his answer, so he used a boat. In one of the most famous passages in his book *Dialogue Concerning the Two Chief World Systems*, Galileo invites the reader to "shut yourself up with some friend in the main cabin below decks on some large ship . . ." He asks that you bring with you (among other things) a few butterflies, a small bowl of water with fish in it, and a bottle that drips into a bowl beneath it. Watch what happens to your cargo when the ship is at rest: the butterflies flit about, the fish swim, and the bottle of water drips into the bowl beneath it. Now, have the ship proceed in any direction at a constant speed. "You will discover," Galileo writes, "not the least change in all the effects named, nor could you tell from any of them whether the ship was moving or standing still." The laws of motion, Galileo concluded, are the same for any observers moving in a straight line at a constant velocity.

This means that a juggler on Galileo's ship or on an airplane could toss and catch his juggling pins in the same way as a juggler on solid ground. Furthermore, if any physicists happened to be aboard, any motion experiments they performed would give exactly the same results that a physicist working on Earth would get. And those results would be identical to the results obtained by a scientist performing the experiments in a rocket ship traveling away from Earth in a straight line at a constant 100,000 miles (160,934 km) per hour. Later chapters will address what would happen in those experiments if the airplane or spaceship were to speed up, slow down, or change direction.

Of course, airplanes and rocket ships traveling at constant velocity are not stationary to an observer on Earth. They are moving. The motion that an observer (or instrument) detects depends on the observer's **frame of reference**. A frame of reference is simply your immediate surroundings, things that are participating in the same motion you are. When you are in the cabin of an airplane, you are in the plane's frame of reference, and unless you look out a window, the plane seems motionless. However, to an observer in a different frame of reference—say one standing on Earth's surface—the plane is moving at 500 miles (805 km) per hour. The point is that both of these representations of reality are equally valid and depend only on the reference frame chosen.

This conclusion leads to a central tenet of relativity: If two or more reference frames are in uniform motion, that is they are not rotating, and are moving in a straight line with constant velocity,

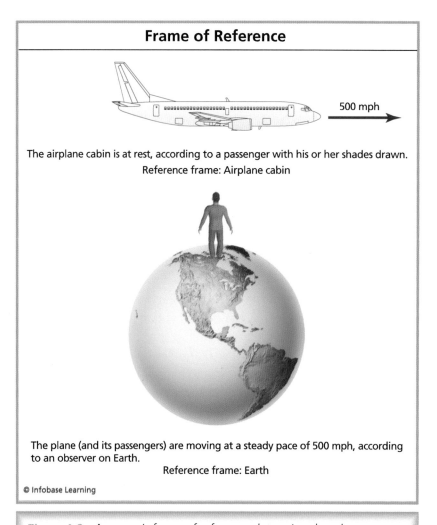

Frame of Reference

500 mph

The airplane cabin is at rest, according to a passenger with his or her shades drawn.
Reference frame: Airplane cabin

The plane (and its passengers) are moving at a steady pace of 500 mph, according to an observer on Earth.
Reference frame: Earth

© Infobase Learning

Figure 1.2   A person's frame of reference determines how he or she experiences motion. The theory of special relativity predicts that time and distance depend on the frame of reference in which they are measured.

then the laws of motion will be the same in all of those frames. In these frames, objects at rest stay at rest, and objects in uniform motion remain in uniform motion unless acted on by a force. Such frames are called **inertial reference frames**, because they are not accelerating or rotating. With this definition in mind, the relativity tenet can be restated: In all inertial frames, the laws of motion are the same. It makes no difference if you are in an airplane, a rocket ship, or in a lab on Earth's surface, any motion experiment you carry out in any inertial frame—including juggling—will give the same results.

Yet a reference frame attached to Earth—a physics lab for example—cannot be inertial. After all, Earth is not moving in a straight line but spinning on its own axis while orbiting the Sun. Furthermore, the Sun is whirling around the center of the Milky Way. How can Earth be an inertial reference frame?

In fact, it is not, at least not exactly. However, the effects of Earth's rotational velocity are tiny to the point of being negligible, and the effects due to its rotation about the Sun are even smaller. Consequently, for almost all intents and purposes, Earth acts as an inertial frame of reference.

Two of the main postulates of relativity theory should now be clear:

- Absolute motion does not exist. Objects move only in relation to other objects.
- Any motion experiment carried out entirely within an inertial frame of reference will give exactly the same result in any other inertial reference frame.

These two postulates—the relativity of motion and the unchanging laws of motion in inertial reference frames—are known today as Galilean relativity, in honor of the man who proposed them first.

TIME TRAVEL, PART 1

These seemingly simple ideas of relativity can, when extended, have truly disturbing implications. One of the most disturbing is the twin

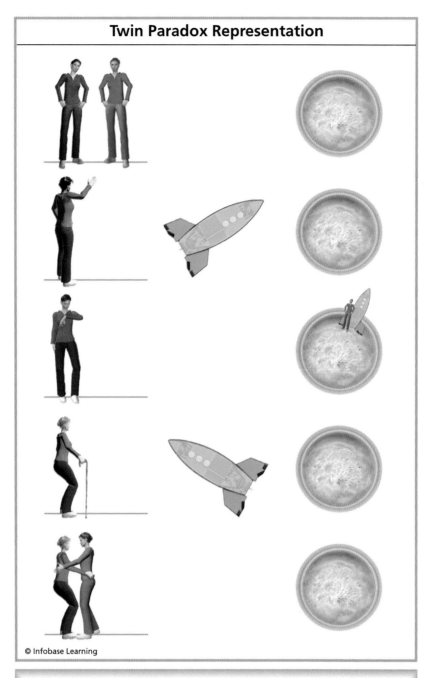

Twin Paradox Representation

© Infobase Learning

Figure 1.3   The twin paradox is a thought experiment in which a twin makes a journey into space in a high-speed rocket and returns home to find she has aged less than her identical twin who stayed on Earth.

paradox. What follows is not science fiction but a consequence of relativity. We will return to this story later, but let us begin with the simplest formulation.

Twin sisters—let's call them Ashley and Betty—live here on Earth. They are nonidentical twins, 25 years old. Ashley is an adventurer who loves to travel, while Betty is a stay-at-home type. Because rocket ships are readily available (at least in this story), Ashley decides to take a trip to a faraway star. She travels fast, close to the speed of light, about 186,000 miles per second (300,000 kilometers per second, or km s^{-1}). Ashley enjoys the sights along the way, but she misses her sister. So, upon reaching her destination, she immediately turns around and starts back, again traveling at close to the speed of light.

Betty meets her at the spaceport. The first thing Ashley notices is the gray streaks in her sister's hair and her slightly sagging skin. When the twins stand side by side, it is clear they are no longer the same age. Betty is years older than Ashley. Ashley has traveled into the future—the future that awaits her as she ages.

This is surprising, but the twin's story is based on factual science. The laws of relativity allow for this kind of time travel. Furthermore, the paradox in the story is not about time travel itself but something else, something related to the relativity of motion, which we will come back to when we revisit the twins' story.

NEWTON'S REVOLUTION

The man who developed the laws that expanded and quantified Galileo's work was English physicist Isaac Newton. He was born in England on Christmas day in 1642, the year Galileo died. Newton was a driven man, a workaholic. When absorbed in a problem, he would forget to eat or sleep, sometimes leaving his evening meal untouched and eating it—cold—for breakfast. His cat grew fat on the uneaten meals delivered to his rooms at the University of Cambridge. Newton had few friends and took no exercise. If he was talking to a guest and a thought came into his head, he might leave the room to be found later "at his desk, hunched over his papers . . . guests forgotten." His clothing was often dirty, his wig askew, and his shoes run down. He was—how else to say it?—sloppy.

However, Newton's mind was anything but sloppy; he was one of the great thinkers of all time. Many of his contributions to astronomy and the science of motion appeared in his 1687 masterwork *The Principia*. It is arguably the most important science book ever written.

Newton starts by defining terms: mass, motion, and force. He follows this with three of the most basic laws of physics, now known as Newton's laws of motion:

- Every body perseveres in its state of being at rest or of moving uniformly straight forward, except insofar as it is compelled to change its state by forces impressed.

Figure 1.4 Isaac Newton was the first person to develop a quantitative understanding of gravity. While it is not clear how he came up with his law of universal gravitation, the popular legend has young Newton sitting beneath an apple tree and wondering if the force that pulled the apple to the earth was the same force that held the Moon in its orbit.

- A change in motion is proportional to the motive force impressed and takes place along the straight line in which that force is impressed. This law can be stated in mathematical form as $F = ma$, where F is the force acting on an object, m is its mass, and a is the acceleration produced when force F acts on an object with mass m.
- To any action, there is always an opposite and equal reaction. In other words, the action of two bodies upon each other are always equal and always opposite in direction.

This was considered genius. People had been puzzling over how things moved and why for millennia. Galileo had anticipated the first law, but no one else had even come close to getting at these truths before Newton. Here, summarized in a few simple sentences, were the answers to questions that had stumped mankind for millennia.

In addition to supplying science with his laws of motion, Newton produced one of the world's most useful equations. It expressed the law of **universal gravitation** and solved a puzzle that had baffled observers of the heavens since humans first gazed at the night sky. Applying it enabled astronomers to finally understand and predict the motions of heavenly bodies.

$$F = \frac{Gm_1m_2}{d^2}$$

In this equation, F is the force of attraction between two objects; m_1 and m_2 are their masses, d is the distance between their centers of mass, and G is the gravitational constant. Newton's law of gravity would stand unchallenged for more than 200 years until Einstein created a more general theory to replace it: relativity.

WHAT ABOUT LIGHT?

After establishing the laws of motion and gravity, Newton tackled another problem that had long stymied science: how to characterize light? As he proceeded, some of his experiments took strange twists. In one bizarre procedure, he took a thin, blunt probe and inserted it "betwixt my eye & the bone." Newton faithfully recorded the results:

The Clockwork Universe

By the early eighteenth century, scientists realized they could use Newton's laws of motion and gravity to predict the behavior of every object in the universe. All they needed to know was what forces were acting on the objects, their mass, and their position in space. If these data were plugged into Newton's equations, the future of the universe could be determined. The universe, it seemed, was a huge machine—a clockwork.

Obviously, getting a detailed description of every particle in the universe is unrealistic—but it is theoretically possible. This realization provoked a question: What place does God have in a clockwork universe, a place where everything is predetermined? Most people accepted that God wound the clock and started it ticking. However, if the universe was predictable after that point, if the clock simply ticked on in a mechanical way, what was left for God to do? Not much, according to some of the great scientists of the day. When the famous French mathematician Pierre-Simon Laplace was asked by Napoleon why he had not mentioned God in his latest book, he supposedly replied, "Sir, I have no need of that hypothesis."

The development of the **quantum theory** at the beginning of the twentieth century deflated the determinism of the earlier era. A new vision of the universe, one based on the probabilities and uncertainties of the quantum world, gradually replaced the clockwork view of the cosmos that grew out of the physics of Galileo and Newton.

"There appeared a great broade blewish darke circle." Exactly what scientific conclusions Newton drew from stabbing his own eyeball is unclear, but his later, thankfully painless, work with prisms solved a problem that had long vexed mankind. White light, Newton discovered, was not a single color but a mixture of all the colors in the visible spectrum.

This work led Newton to suspect that light was a particle. The crucial test of that hypothesis was left to English scientist Thomas Young who disagreed with Newton's findings and performed a set of experiments in the early nineteenth century to show that light was a wave. This key experiment is known as the double slit experiment.

In this experiment, light passes through a single slit or pinhole and continues on through a double slit. The result is a series of alternating light and dark bands called an interference pattern. This pattern occurs because of the way in which waves behave. When the peaks or troughs of two light waves coincide, the result is a bright band of light; when the peak of one wave coincides with trough of another, the waves cancel each other and produce a dark band. Particles, however, do not produce peaks and troughs, so this interference pattern could not appear if light was a particle.

Another step toward determining the nature of light was to measure its speed. One of the first scientists to try to do this was Galileo. His idea was to have two people, each with a lantern equipped with a shutter, stand apart from each other at a distance of a mile or more. The first person would open the shutter of his lamp. When the second person saw the light, he would quickly open the shutter of his

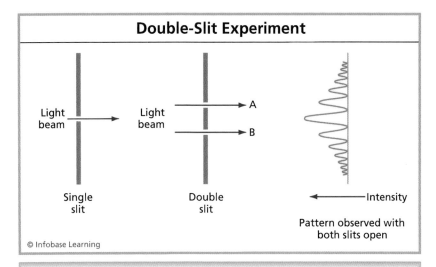

Double-Slit Experiment

Light beam

Single slit

Light beam

Double slit

A

B

Intensity

Pattern observed with both slits open

© Infobase Learning

Figure 1.5 The double-slit experiment provided proof that light was a wave.

What Is the Real Speed of Light?

Although we have so far presented the speed of light as a large, unchanging number, there is no such thing as "the real speed of light." The speed light varies with the substance through which it travels. The speed of light usually quoted is 186,282 miles per second, or 299,792 kilometers per second (km s^{-1}). This is the speed of light in a vacuum, usually designated by the letter c and rounded off to a zippy 186,000 miles per second or 300,000 km s^{-1}.

However, light moves at a slower speed when it passes through substances. Although its speed in air is almost the same as its speed in a vacuum, less transparent materials slow it down. The index of refraction of a substance is the ratio of the speed of light in a vacuum, c, to the speed of light through that substance. The index of refraction of some common substances is given below.

Index of Refraction

Substance	Index of Refraction
Vacuum	1.000
Air	1.0003
Water	1.33
Flint glass	1.66
Diamond	2.42

Thus, the speed of light in a diamond would be $c/2.42 = 123,881$ km s^{-1}

Light travels even slower when passing through substances with atoms that are packed more densely than the atoms in diamonds. In one experiment, the passage of light through super-cooled sodium was measured at a stately 38 miles (61 kilometers) an hour, about the speed of rush hour traffic.

For our needs, the phrase *speed of light* will mean the speed of light in a vacuum, unless otherwise stated.

own lantern. The elapsed time between the first person's opening his shutter and seeing the light from the second person's lantern divided into twice the distance between the men would be the speed of light. Unfortunately, when Galileo tried this experiment, the results were inconclusive. Light traveled too fast to be measured in this crude fashion.

The first solid estimate of the speed of light came 50 years later from Danish astronomer Olaus Roemer. Using astronomical observations, he calculated a speed of 132,000 miles per second (about 212,000 km s^{-1}). Roemer's measurement was bit off the mark, and it was not until 1862 that another scientist came up with a measurement that was close to the actual speed of light. The man who did this was Jean Foucault, a French physicist who was famous for building a special pendulum that detected the rotation of Earth. Using an ingenious set up of rotating and fixed mirrors, Foucault measured a speed of 185,000 miles (297,729 km) per second, not far from today's accepted value of 186,282 miles per second (299,792 km s^{-1}).

Of course, knowing that light was a wave and measuring its speed was only part of what was needed to understand the nature of light. The key question had yet to be answered: Exactly what was light, anyway? The answer would come from yet another brilliant physicist, a Scotsman named James Clerk Maxwell. He made a discovery that was a crucial step in the march toward the theory of relativity.

2

Maxwell Sees the Light

I n the spring of 1820, Danish philosopher turned scientist Hans Christian Ørsted (often written as Oersted, in English) was giving a private lecture to advanced students at the University of Copenhagen. He had attached a platinum wire to a voltaic pile (a primitive battery). By chance (or maybe on purpose, as he later claimed), a compass was placed underneath the wire with the needle parallel to the wire. When Ørsted closed the circuit, he noticed that the compass needle moved.

Later experiments with a stronger battery showed that a compass placed beneath a wire with the needle aligned with the wire would swing 90° when a current was flowing. Furthermore, when the compass was placed above the wire, the needle would again swing to an angle of 90° from the wire, but the poles were reversed. If the needle pointed north when the compass was beneath the wire, then it pointed south when it was placed above it.

Ørsted published his results a few months later. He announced that an electric current flowing in a wire creates a circular **magnetic field**. This accounted for the compass's reversing direction when it was moved from below the wire to above it.

LINKING ELECTRICITY AND MAGNETISM

Although scientists had long suspected that electricity was somehow related to magnetism, Ørsted's experiment was the first direct

Figure 2.1 Hans Christian Ørsted demonstrates the properties of electromagnetism.

evidence of that connection. The key to his discovery was Alessandro Volta's invention of a battery that could be used for laboratory experiments. Surprisingly, more than 20 years passed between that invention and Ørsted's crucial discovery. Scientists of the day lamented the delay, but they knew what caused it. The prominent physicist Charles Augustin de Coulomb (1736–1806) believed that electricity and magnetism were distinct, unrelated phenomena. Coulomb was so influential that many scientists subscribed to this view, long after his death. When a visiting physicist spoke of uniting the two, shortly after Ørsted's announcement, one scientist recalled that his ideas "were rejected. . . . Everyone decided that they were impossible."

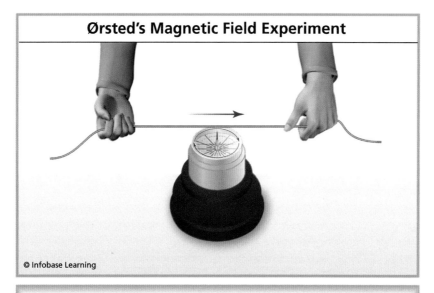

Figure 2.2 Ørsted discovered that a wire carrying an electric current affected a magnetic needle, causing it to move to a position perpendicular to the direction of the wire. When the wire was placed under the needle, it pointed in the opposite direction, indicating a circular magnetic field around wire.

Negative reactions to new data and new theories are common in science. The most prominent scientists of any generation are usually older men and women who attained their status because of their good ideas. They naturally resist new hypotheses that might replace those ideas. In science, though, right makes might. The best ideas eventually win out. After Coulomb's death, his influence waned, and scientists began to eagerly explore the link between electricity and magnetism.

News of Ørsted's discovery raced across Europe. Within months, physicists had quantified the relationship between electricity and magnetism. Then, a year later, the marvelously intuitive English experimentalist Michael Faraday cobbled together the world's first electric motor. Faraday's second big invention took 10 years longer.

After Ørsted's experiments, it was clear that an electric current could create a magnetic field. Indeed, Faraday found he could pass a current through a coil of wire wrapped around an iron core and create an electromagnet. Did it not makes sense, he wondered, that

Figure 2.3 Michael Faraday's most significant contributions to science were his experimental research on electricity, the details of which were published over the course of 40 years, and his discoveries of the laws of electromagnetic induction and the laws of electrolysis.

if electricity could produce a magnet that a magnet could produce electricity?

Faraday gave this idea his best shot. He arranged magnets and wires in every conceivable way, but he could not generate a current. Finally, in 1831, he began a series of fruitful experiments. When the switch is closed, a current flows through the coil connected to the battery. This magnetizes the iron ring. Faraday hoped that the magnetized iron ring would induce an electric current in the second coil that would cause the compass needle to move.

The initial results of this effort were disappointing. As before, the indicator needle did not budge while the current flowed. However, Faraday noticed that at the instant he closed the circuit, the magnetized needle twitched. Furthermore, when he opened the circuit, shutting off the current, the needle wobbled again. In between the closing and opening of the circuit, the needle was stationary.

Faraday soon figured out what was happening. It was not magnetism itself that generated current, it was the change in magnetism. Closing the switch changed the magnetism of the iron ring from

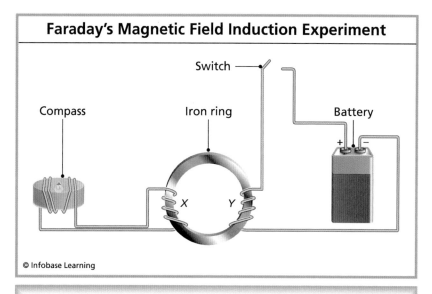

Faraday's Magnetic Field Induction Experiment

Switch

Compass   Iron ring   Battery

X   Y

© Infobase Learning

Figure 2.4   When Faraday closed the switch, a current passed through the first coil (y). The iron ring became magnetized and the compass needle attached to the second coil (x) deflected momentarily.

zero to some value, producing an electric current in the second coil. Opening the switch also produced a change in magnetism.

This principle, called electromagnetic induction, is used today in the electric generators that provide power to our homes and factories. A source of energy, such as coal, natural gas, or falling water, spins wire coils in the presence of a magnet. The rotating coils experience a changing magnetic field and generate an electric current, just as Faraday discovered.

Electricity, Faraday knew, was the movement of electrical charges. Benjamin Franklin had deduced that years earlier. (However, the carrier of those charges would remain unknown until 1897 when British physicist J.J. Thomson announced his discovery of the electron.) By the middle of the eighteenth century, Faraday's work, along with that of Øersted and other scientists, had added a great deal of knowledge to Franklin's early observations. That knowledge could be summarized in the following four neat, qualitative statements about electricity and magnetism:

- Two types of electric charges exist, which Franklin had labeled as positive and negative. Charged objects exert forces on one another. Opposite charges attract; like charges repel.
- Magnets also exert forces on one another.
- A current of moving electrical charges induces magnetism.
- Changing magnetism produces an electric current.

In addition to performing experiments to determine (or confirm) these facts, Faraday was beginning to think about electricity and magnetism in an entirely different way from his predecessors. It involved a new concept, one that visualized how forces might look in space.

FIELDS

Magnets produce a field, or so you were told earlier in this chapter. However, the word "field" has never been precisely defined. This concept in relativity, and other areas of physics, is so important that it is worth exploring more deeply.

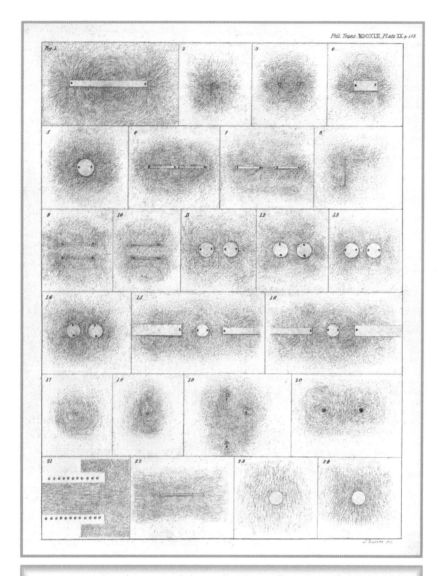

Phil. Trans. MDCCCLII, *Plate* IX. p.168

Figure 2.5 Faraday created these diagrams of magnetic fields around various configurations of magnets. The drawings were published in the *Philosophical Transactions of the Royal Society* in 1852.

One of the more disturbing implications of Newton's law of universal gravitation is that it demands that two bodies reach out across empty space to attract one another. This action-at-a-distance property bothered Newton. He finally gave up trying to explain it. "I have not as yet been able," he wrote in his 1687 book *Principia*, "to deduce from phenomena the reason for these properties of gravity, and I do not feign hypotheses."

The same problem baffled Faraday in his thinking about magnets and electrical currents. To him, Øersted's result, as well as his own experiments, posed a question similar to the one that baffled Newton. How could an electric current reach across space to deflect a compass needle? Furthermore, how could changing the magnetism of an iron bar induce a current in an unattached wire?

Unlike Newton, Faraday was no mathematical genius. He was brilliant in a different way. Faraday was a highly visual person who saw the world in terms of drawings. He began to imagine lines of force radiating from a magnet. Those lines of force influence some objects (iron filings, for instance), arranging them in a familiar pattern.

Faraday dramatically extended the field concept. Lines of force, he hypothesized, are not limited to magnets but are also created by electric charges and currents. The lines of electric force can be thought of as straight lines beginning in the center of an object and extending into the space around it. Electric lines of force attract or repel charged particles. In Figure 2.6, the lines of force are represented by arrows. The arrows are **vectors** with the direction of an arrow representing the direction of the force and its length representing its magnitude.

By adding motion to Faraday's field concept, we can restate two of the statements on which electricity and magnetism were based in the middle of the eighteenth century:

  * Moving electric charges create a magnetic field.
  * A changing magnetic field creates an **electric field**.

Thanks largely to Michael Faraday's experimental work and insights, the linkage between electricity and magnetism was emerging. Still, one might ask, what do these advances in electricity and magnetism have to do with our understanding of light, which was crucial to Einstein's development of relativity theory? As it turns out, quite a bit.

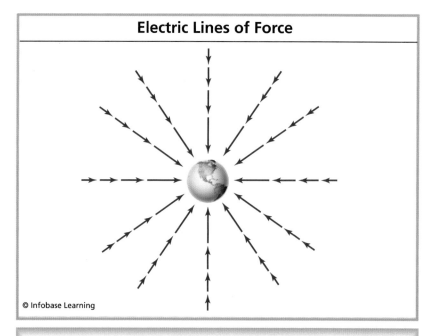

Electric Lines of Force

© Infobase Learning

Figure 2.6 This illustration represents a field for a negatively charged particle. The length of each arrow gives the strength of the field at that point, and the arrows point in the direction of the field.

ELECTRICITY AND LIGHT

Although Scottish physicist James Clerk Maxwell is not as widely acclaimed, as Newton or Einstein, many physicists believe that his scientific achievements were equal to theirs. His contributions are found in every aspect of modern life. In fact, the entire electronics industry can be said to exist because of him. Maxwell took the work of Faraday and others and wrapped it up in a tight mathematical package. His work also answered the question that had long stumped humankind: Exactly what is light, anyway?

Maxwell's package was a set of four equations. The equations are beautiful to those who can understand the advanced math. You can easily find these equations in most university science departments. They are listed on geeky T-shirts worn by some physics majors.

Maxwell's initial formulation of his equations reflected much of what was known about electricity and magnetism at the time. A

Figure 2.7   James Clerk Maxwell developed electromagnetic theory from previously unrelated observations and equations involving electricity, magnetism, and optics.

moving electric charge produces a magnetic field. A changing magnetic field produces an electric field. Maxwell noticed a certain lack of symmetry in those two statements: What about changing electric fields? Should they not produce a magnetic field? Of course, they

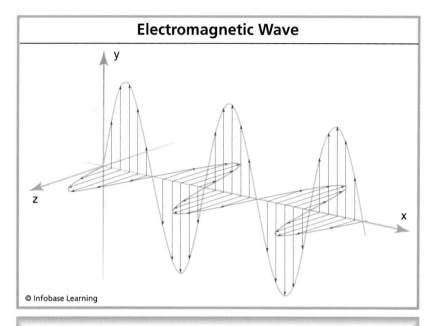

Electromagnetic Wave

© Infobase Learning

Figure 2.8   This illustration shows an electromagnetic wave propagating in positive x direction. The vectors of the electric field (red) are parallel to the y axis, while the vectors of the magnetic field (blue) are parallel to the z axis.

should, Maxwell concluded. In a leap of genius, he added a new term to his equations to reflect another way to create a magnetic field.

Its inclusion led Maxwell to a startling insight: If a changing electric field produces a magnetic field, and a changing magnetic field produces an electric field, then what happens if you take an electrically charged particle and begin to shake it? The changing electric field generates a magnetic field, which generates a changing electric field, which generates a changing magnetic field—and so on and so on and so on.

The result, a self-perpetuating system of alternating electric and magnetic fields that are perpendicular to one another, is called an electromagnetic wave. These waves (Figure 2.8) have energy but no mass. The energy originates with the vibrating charge. In an isolated system, the vibrations will slow and eventually stop unless energy is added. This is easy to visualize: Think of a ball attached to a stiff spring; hold the bottom of the spring in one hand and whack the ball

Maxwell's Equations

Maxwell's four equations are some of the most beautiful and daunting in physics. They were even more daunting when Maxwell first laid them out. His original formulation included not four equations but twenty. Oliver Heaviside, a brilliant self-taught engineer, reduced Maxwell's original twenty to the compact mathematical expressions that will fit on a T-shirt.

To use Maxwell's equations for solving practical problems requires knowledge of **vector calculus**. Fortunately, it is possible to distill the meaning of the equations without actually solving them. We will do this by focusing on the simplest form of the equations, the form used by Basil Mahon in his biography of Maxwell, *The Man Who Changed Everything*. Mahon makes the general equations more manageable by applying them to a point in empty space. Here, then, are Maxwell's famous equations:

$$\text{div } \boldsymbol{E} = 0$$

$$\text{div } \boldsymbol{H} = 0$$

$$\text{curl } \boldsymbol{E} = -\left(\frac{1}{v}\right)\frac{\partial H}{\partial t}$$

$$\text{curl } \boldsymbol{H} = \left(\frac{1}{v}\right)\frac{\partial H}{\partial t}$$

Symbols in boldface indicate that the variable is a vector quantity, which has both direction and magnitude. $\boldsymbol{E}$ is the electric force; $\boldsymbol{H}$ is the magnetic force. The term *div* is an abbreviation for divergence, (sometimes represented as ∇F). It is a measure of the vector forces near the point and is roughly related to the tendency of a force to be directed inward or outward. Curl is a measure of the tendency of a force to loop around on itself, as magnetic fields do. The terms $\partial \boldsymbol{H}/\partial t$ and $\partial \boldsymbol{E}/\partial t$ are **partial derivatives**: They specify how the magnetic and electric forces change with time.

(continues)

(continued)

The first equation says that the electric force in the space around the point is zero, meaning no charge is present. The second equation says the same thing for the magnetic force. Equation three shows how changes in the magnetic force affect the electric force. Number four specifies how changes in the electric force affect the magnetic force.

Taken together, the equations paint a picture of a wave of alternating electric and magnetic fields moving at velocity v, which turned out to be the speed of light.

with the other hand; the ball will swing back and forth with decreasing amplitude until it finally stops, its energy dissipated. In atomic and subatomic systems, the ball might carry a charge, and its energy would be dissipated as electromagnetic radiation.

One of the great surprises of Maxwell's equations came from a calculation made by Maxwell himself. Using fundamental relationships, he determined the speed of these newly identified electromagnetic waves. When he did the arithmetic, he came up with a speed of 193,085 miles per second (310,740 km s^{-1}). One can imagine Maxwell's happy astonishment. Like all good physicists of the day, he was aware that the speed of light in air had been experimentally determined to be 195,639 miles per second (314,850 km s^{-1}). Light, Maxwell immediately realized, was an electromagnetic wave. (More accurate measurements made later came up with today's accepted value of the speed of light in a vacuum as 186,282 miles per second, or 299,792 km s^{-1}.)

Maxwell presented his work on electricity, magnetism, and light to the Royal Society in 1864 and published it a year later. It scarcely rippled the scientific waters. According to Mahon, "most of his contemporaries were bemused. It was almost as if Einstein had popped out of a time machine to tell them about **general relativity**: they simply did not know what to make of it."

Despite its lukewarm initial reception, Maxwell's theory is regarded today as one of the greatest achievements in science. It explains all electromagnetic phenomena; it tells us much about the nature of light; and it opened the door that led scientists to the other types of electromagnetic radiation that are used today: microwaves, X-rays, and radio waves to name a few. More than 20 years after Maxwell's breakthrough, Heinrich Hertz produced and detected electromagnetic waves. Ever since, scientists and engineers have used Maxwell's ideas and his equations in many important ways, from creating delicate, high-precision instruments to the construction of immense electric dynamos.

THE ETHER

Scientists had known that light was a wave since Young's 1801 double-slit experiment. Furthermore, thanks to Maxwell, they now knew that those waves were electromagnetic waves. Light's speed in a vacuum was also well established. The nature of light seemed pinned down well enough, except for one problem. As Galileo pointed out, all motion is relative. In that case, what was the speed of light relative to?

Waves, the thinking went, must have a medium to propagate through. The speed of the waves is relative to that medium. When a pebble is dropped into a pool of water, the resulting waves will spread across the surface in every direction. The medium of propagation is the water, and the speed of the wave is relative to the water. The usual medium for sound waves is air. When one speaks of the speed of sound, they most often mean its speed relative to air molecules. Take away air—its medium of propagation—and sound vanishes. You can yell all you want in a vacuum, but no one will hear you.

So, what medium transmitted light waves? Most nineteenth-century scientists thought that the answer was the ether (sometimes called the **luminiferous ether**). The idea of an ether had been around even before Newton. Its properties had to be unlike any other substance. It had to be a fluid to fill space and carry waves. It also had to be massless and without viscosity so that it would not affect the motions of the planets, which followed Newton's laws with no correction needed for an ether. It also had to be completely transparent because the light from the stars reached our eyes after traveling millions of miles across space.

No such substance was known to exist, but the idea of the ether persisted until 1887 (and beyond in the case of a few hard-to-convince scientists) when two U.S. physicists devised an elaborate experiment to demonstrate its existence.

An Ingenious Apparatus

The theory at the time of the Michelson-Morley experiment was that the ether was stationary, an absolute reference frame that extended throughout the universe. However, the Earth is moving: rotating on its own axis, orbiting the Sun, swinging around the Milky Way. The motion of the Earth through the ether should create what was called the ether wind. Because of the wind, one should be able to measure different speeds for light depending on the direction of Earth's motion through the ether. Light traveling in the same direction as the ether wind should have a higher speed than light shining into the ether wind.

Because light moves so fast, a direct measurement and comparison of its speed under different conditions was impossible. The Michelson interferometer was designed to detect small differences in its speed. Light from a source is divided by a beam splitter. Half of the light follows one path; the other half follows a path that is perpendicular to the first path (Figure 2.9). The beams are recombined in the last leg of their journey.

If both beams travel at the same speed, the result is a series of light and dark bands called interference fringes. The fringes arise from regions of constructive and destructive interference in the recombined light beam. If the speed of one of the light beams were to change, the experimenters knew it would shift the interference fringes, thereby proving the existence of the ether. By adjusting the orientation of the apparatus, the scientists hoped to detect differences in the speeds of the two perpendicular light beams caused by changes in the interferometer's

American scientists Albert Michelson and Edward Morley set out to directly detect the existence of the ether. The 1887 experiment, arguably the most famous in all of science, is now universally referred to as the Michelson-Morley experiment. The work was

position relative to the ether wind. Of course, no significant shift in the interference fringes was ever observed, regardless of how the apparatus was oriented.

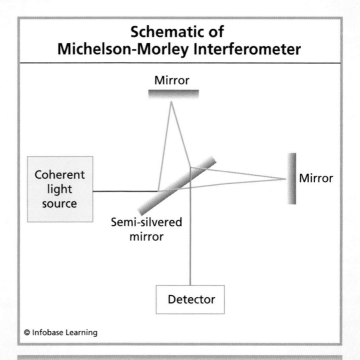

Figure 2.9 The Michelson-Morley experiment depended on Michelson's *interferometer*, a sensitive optical tool that compares the optical path lengths for light moving in two mutually perpendicular directions. It was theorized that, if the speed of light were constant with respect to the ether through which Earth was moving, that motion could be detected by comparing the speed of light in the direction of Earth's motion and the speed of light at right angles to Earth's motion.

difficult and delicate. An interferometer was floated in a pool of mercury to minimize vibration. The results, which were checked and double-checked, shocked the experimenters and the scientific community. No ether could be detected.

Michelson, Morley, and most other scientists of that day believed in the existence of the ether. They also believed that the Michelson-Morley experiment would demonstrate its existence. Thus, one of the most famous experiments in the history of science gave a negative result. However, this result did clear the air: There is no ether, and the speed of light in a vacuum is always about 186,000 miles per second (300,000 km s^{-1}). Albert Einstein would use this new discovery to blow away many of mankind's long-held concepts of space and time.

3

Einstein's Miracle Year

By the beginning of 1905, the 25-year-old Albert Einstein was coming off a personal low. A few years earlier he had been broke and unemployed. He had fathered an out-of-wedlock child with his longtime girlfriend, an event that severely strained their relationship. However, as 1905 got underway, his life was on the upswing. He had a job at the patent office in Bern, Switzerland, and had recently received a raise. He had married his girlfriend, fathered another child, and was settling into domestic life. However, Einstein's life was about to change direction again—dramatically, and unexpectedly.

No one could have guessed that on January 1, the dapper, curly-haired patent clerk was about to rebuild the foundations of science and begin a journey that would make him the best-known scientist on the planet. In the coming months, he would publish three revolutionary papers, any one of which would have made him famous. Taken together, they constitute Einstein's "miracle year," a year that will likely never be duplicated.

Einstein's first two papers were unrelated to relativity, but they had a huge effect on how scientists understand the world. They are briefly summarized here to acquaint the reader with those discoveries and illustrate Einstein's approach to science.

Figure 3.1 Albert Einstein is shown at age 26 in 1905.

PHOTOELECTRIC EFFECT

The first paper answered a question that was bedeviling scientists of the day. It first arose in 1887 when, during an experiment, the German physicist Heinrich Hertz noticed that an electric spark jumped the gap between two electrodes more readily when a light was shined on them. Hertz had no idea why this happened. Later experiments showed that shining a light on a metal cathode could cause a current to flow across an air gap. After the discovery of the electron and the realization that it is the carrier of electricity, scientists showed that the current could jump the gap because light was knocking electrons out of the metal. Shining electromagnetic radiation on a metal cathode to produce or amplify an electric current is called the **photoelectric effect**.

Surprisingly, when experimentalists increased the intensity of the light by moving it closer to the cathode, they found that the energy of the electrons emitted did not increase. Higher-intensity light dislodged more electrons, but none of them had more energy than electrons that had been knocked out by lower-intensity light.

This was a bewildering result. Thomas Young's experiments had clearly shown that light was a wave. Classical wave mechanics predicted that increasing the intensity of light would increase the amount of energy hitting the cathode. Therefore, that should increase the energy of the dislodged electrons. However, higher-energy electrons were produced only when the frequency of the light was increased, not its intensity.

Einstein solved the conundrum by following up on Max Planck's conjecture about the discontinuous nature of the energy emitted by a blackbody. Einstein suggested that light came in tiny indivisible packets of energy called **quanta**. One could calculate the energy of the packets using the equation developed by Planck, which relates a wave's energy to its frequency according the equation $E = hf$. In this equation, E is the energy of the packet, h is Planck's constant, and f is the frequency of the incident light.

If Planck was correct, Einstein reasoned, then making the light more intense would increase the number of packets (later named **photons**) striking the cathode, but it would not increase the energy of any individual packet. More packets would knock more electrons out of the metal, but the energy of the dislodged electrons would not increase. One could raise the energy of the knocked-out electrons only by boosting the energy of the packets. This could be done by increasing the frequency of the light. This, of course, was exactly what experiments showed. Einstein had quantized light—and explained the photoelectric effect.

Einstein was awarded the 1921 Nobel Prize in physics for this breakthrough. For almost any other scientist, his work on the photoelectric effect would have been the high point of a career, but Einstein was only getting started.

BROWNIAN MOTION

Robert Brown was a Scottish botanist and an accomplished microscopist. In 1827, he suspended grains of pollen in water and, watching them through his microscope, found that "they were very evidently in motion." The motion he observed was a random jiggling of the pollen, which was later named **Brownian motion.** He satisfied himself that the movement of the grains was not due to currents or eddies in the water, but he was unable to determine what caused the jiggling.

No one else could explain it either, and so matters stood until Einstein published the second big paper of his miracle year. His first sentence went right to the heart of the matter: "In this paper," he wrote, "it will be shown that, according to the molecular-kinetic theory of heat, bodies of a microscopically visible size suspended in liquids must, as a result of thermal molecular motions, perform motions of such magnitudes that they can be easily observed with a microscope." In other words, the random movement of water molecules bumping against the pollen grains caused Brownian motion.

By the time Einstein's paper appeared, many scientists had accepted the atomic hypothesis, but some had not. Einstein's interpretation of the cause of Brownian motion showed conclusively that molecules—and, by inference, atoms—must exist.

TOWARD RELATIVITY

These two papers nicely illustrate Einstein's approach to science. First, neither paper presented new experimental data. Einstein was a theorist. His work was done in his office or on his sailboat, not in a lab. Second, Einstein thought big. He took pains to explain that he did not set out to account for either the photoelectric effect or Brownian motion. His goal was grander. He wanted to know how the universe worked.

He wondered how light would act if energy came in quanta and what statistical mechanics tells us about the interaction of atoms and molecules with small particles of matter. Of course, Einstein was aware that his work might solve the problems posed by the photoelectric effect or explain Brownian motion. However, his principal motivation, he claimed, was not to examine inconsistencies in a theory but to explain the workings of the universe based on the fundamental axioms of physics.

Finally, in these papers and in later ones, Einstein was careful to propose quantitative theories that could be experimentally tested. In fact, he often suggested experiments himself.

With those two papers behind him, Einstein started to dig into a problem that had long bothered him. Years before, when he was 16 years old, he tried to imagine what would happen if he could run alongside a beam of light. Using Maxwell's description of electromagnetic radiation, he later concluded that he would see a "field at rest though spatially oscillating. There seems to be no such thing, however, neither on the basis of experience nor according to Maxwell's equations."

In other words, observers in one frame of reference who are watching a beam of light while standing on Earth would see an entirely different wave than the frozen wave seen by a person in the reference frame of the light beam. Einstein was skeptical of this conclusion, but did not have a better idea. "[I]n this paradox," he said, "the germ of the **special relativity** theory is already contained."

Exactly how that germ grew into relativity theory is still being discussed by historians of science. However, by 1905, it is clear that Einstein recognized a huge crack in the structure of science. Galileo had pointed out long before Einstein that all motion is relative. In addition, one could use Maxwell's equations to calculate the speed of light as 186,000 miles per second (300,000 km s^{-1}). However, Maxwell's equations do not specify what that speed is relative to. So, that created a big question. The speed of light is 186,000 miles per second (300,000 km s^{-1}), but *relative to what*?

The answer to that question, many scientists believed, was the luminiferous ether. The speed of light would always be the same relative to the ether. Thus, one would always measure the same speed for light in any reference frame that is stationary relative to the ether.

It would seem that the key Einstein used to open the door to relativity must have been the Michelson-Morley experiment, which indicated that there was no ether. This would have forced him to consider what the speed of light was relative to. Einstein, however, was ambivalent about the experiment's effect on his thinking. On one occasion, he said he had read about the Michelson-Morley experiment only *after* he proposed his theory.

In any case, Einstein decided that Maxwell's laws were correct and that light must travel at the same speed in all reference frames in uniform motion. This seemingly simple conclusion led Einstein to the central tenet of special relativity: *The laws of physics are the same for observers in all inertial reference frames.*

This principle extended the Galilean relativity of motion to all the laws of physics, including those of Maxwell. It also answered a question that had bothered the young Einstein. What would you see if you could run at 186,000 miles per second (300,000 km s^{-1}) beside a light beam? He now knew the answer. You would see an electromagnetic wave moving at 186,000 miles per second (300,000 km s^{-1}) relative to you. This seemingly simple conclusion leads to amazing consequences. Time, for instance, is not what it seems to be.

TIME DILATION

Let us begin exploring special relativity with a simple thought experiment. Consider a box 186,000 miles (300,000 km) tall (Figure 3.2). Install a light flash emitter and a detector at the bottom of the box and a mirror at the top. Pump out the air. Activate the flash, and an observer—let's assign this job to our space-traveling twin Ashley, who is back from her journey—measures the elapsed time. Because the speed of light in a vacuum is 186,000 miles per second (300,000 km s^{-1}), two seconds will pass between emission and detection.

Now, look at the same box and the same two events from the perspective of another observer. Ashley's twin Betty is standing outside the box, as shown in Figure 3.2B. The box is moving in a

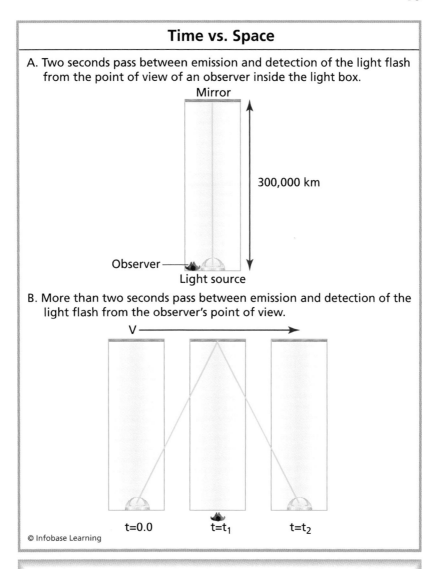

Time vs. Space

A. Two seconds pass between emission and detection of the light flash from the point of view of an observer inside the light box.

Mirror

300,000 km

Observer

Light source

B. More than two seconds pass between emission and detection of the light flash from the observer's point of view.

V

t=0.0   t=t₁   t=t₂

© Infobase Learning

Figure 3.2   The elapsed time between two events depends on the reference frame of the observer.

straight line with velocity *v* relative to Betty. At t = 0, the flash goes off. The light beam hits the mirror and returns to the detector at t = t₁. This is the same light box, the same flash, the same two events shown in Figure 3.2A. However, from Betty's perspective, the light beam travels farther than it did in Ashley's frame of reference. Recall Einstein's conclusion that the speed of light is the same in all uniformly moving reference frames. Because the light must travel farther in Betty's frame of reference, she will measure a longer time between flash and detection than Ashley will.

This leads to a disquieting conclusion. The elapsed time between the two events depends on the reference frame of the observer. This stretching of time is called **time dilation**. It is a property of time itself and is independent of the clock used to measure it. Try the same experiment using an atomic clock or your wristwatch. The result will be the same. "Moving clocks run slower" is the phrase often used to remember which clock measures the shorter time between events. Ashley—who is in the reference frame where the events take place— will always measure a shorter time than Betty. Furthermore, there is no "correct" time. Both measurements of the elapsed time are equally valid. Time is not absolute. It depends on your frame of reference.

WAS NEWTON WRONG?

Time was a fixed quantity to Isaac Newton. It was the same through-out the universe. "Absolute . . . time," he wrote, "in and of itself and of its own nature, without reference to anything external, flows uni-formly. . . ." Einstein showed that Newton was wrong. Absolute time does not exist. Time is relative. It depends on the reference frame in which it is measured, as demonstrated in the thought experiment with the moving box. Still, how could Newton be wrong? His concepts of space and time have been, and continue to be, applied to all sorts of problems, and they consistently give the right answers. A simple cal-culation involving Ashley and Betty will shed light on this mystery.

Using the Pythagorean theorem and a little algebra, one can derive an equation relating the elapsed time of an event as measured by two observers in inertial reference frames moving with respect to one another. Figure 3.3 shows the light box passing Betty at veloc-ity v. The path of the moving light beam forms a triangle. In this example, t_A is the time elapsed between emission and detection of the light beam as measured by Ashley, who is in the box's frame of reference, and t_B is the elapsed time as measured by Betty. The length of the triangle's base is designated as vt_B, which is the velocity of the box relative to Betty multiplied by the time it takes for the beam to leave the emitter and reach the detector.

Time is Relative Experiment

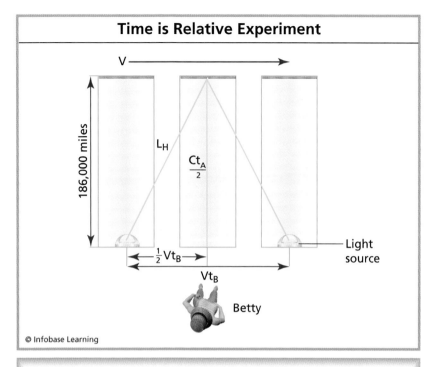

© Infobase Learning

Figure 3.3   From Betty's point of view, the light beam traces a triangle. Using the Pythagorean theorem, one can calculate the distance the light beam travels.

Now, divide the triangle into two identical right triangles. The base of each triangle is then $vt_B/2$. The length of the line dividing the two triangles is the length of the box, which can be expressed as $ct_A/2$, the speed of light multiplied by one-half the time as measured by Ashley who is in the box's frame of reference. (The factor ½ is present because t_A is the time it takes for the light beam to travel from the flash to the detector and back. So, we must divide by 2 to get the one-way distance.) We can now use the Pythagorean theorem to calculate the length of the hypotenuse, which is designated as L_H. Using this equation, we can derive the relationship between the times measured by Ashley and Betty.

$$L_H = \left[\left(\frac{Vt_B}{2} \right)^2 + \left(\frac{ct_A}{2} \right)^2 \right]^{\frac{1}{2}}$$

But L_H equals the speed of light, c, multiplied by the time Betty records for the event, again divided by 2 because the hypotenuse represents only half of the path of the light beam. Thus,

$$L_H = \frac{ct_B}{2}$$

Combining these equations gives

$$\frac{ct_B}{2} = \left[\left(\frac{Vt_B}{2} \right)^2 + \left(\frac{Ct_A}{2} \right)^2 \right]^{1/2}$$

Now square both sides

$$\frac{c^2 t_B^2}{4} = \frac{V^2 t_B^2}{4} + \frac{c^2 t_A^2}{4}$$

Multiply through by 4.

$$c^2 t_B^2 = V^2 t_B^2 + c^2 t_A^2$$

Rearranging gives

$$c^2 t_A^2 = c^2 t_B^2 - V^2 t_B^2$$

or

$$t_A^2 = t_B^2 - t_B^2 \frac{V^2}{c^2}$$

$$t_A^2 = t_B^2 \left(1 - \frac{V^2}{c^2} \right)$$

$$t_A = t_B \left(1 - \frac{V^2}{c^2} \right)^{1/2}$$

Now, let us apply this equation to an example. Suppose Betty is standing beside a highway. Traffic is moving from left to right at a steady 60 miles (97 km) per hour. Off goes the light flash. We know that Ashley will measure a time from flash to detection of exactly 2 seconds. We can calculate how much time Betty would measure. Sixty miles per hour is 0.027 km s^{-1}, so starting with the time-dilation equation and filling in the numbers gives

$$t_A = t_B \left[1 - \frac{v^2}{c^2} \right]^{\frac{1}{2}}$$

$$t_B = \frac{t_A}{\left(1 - \frac{v^2}{c^2} \right)^{\frac{1}{2}}}$$

$$t_B = \frac{2}{\left[1 - \frac{(0.027)^2}{(3 \times 10^5)^2} \right]^{\frac{1}{2}}}$$

$$t_B = \frac{2}{\left[1 - \frac{(7.3 \times 10^{-4})}{(9 \times 10^{10})} \right]^{\frac{1}{2}}}$$

$$t_B = \frac{2}{\left[1 - 8 \times 10^{-15} \right]^{\frac{1}{2}}}$$

Now, 8 x 10^{-15} seconds is a very small number, so the difference between the two measured times is negligible, so t_B = 2 seconds. Even if Ashley was moving at 100,000 miles per hour (45 km s^{-1}), the measured times would be essentially identical. Furthermore, if she speeded up to an incredible 100,000,000 miles per hour (44,700 km s^{-1}), Betty would still measure a time of only 2.02 seconds, a mere 1/200th of a second more than Ashley. So, for inertial reference frames moving at ordinary speeds relative to one another, relativistic effects can be ignored. Newton's laws work just as well as Einstein's, which is why they have stood the tests of time so well.

However, as the relative velocity of the reference frames approaches the speed of light, Einstein and Newton begin to differ. To illustrate this, let us return to the twins' space adventure.

TIME TRAVEL: PART II

Ashley, the adventurous one, is off to see the universe. She heads for a star 25 **light-years** from Earth. Being a bit of a speed demon, she has bought a "muscle" rocket ship, an especially fast vessel that cruises at 270,000 km s^{-1} (604 million miles per hour). In relativity calculations, it is convenient to express speeds as a fraction of the speed of light, and 270,000 km s^{-1} is 0.9 times the speed of light or 0.9c. From Betty's point of view here on Earth, the trip will take 25 light-years divided by her speed expressed as a fraction of the speed of light, which is 25/0.9, or about 28 years.

One can calculate the time elapsed on the space ship using the time-dilation equation. In this example t_A is the time as measured in the space ship by Ashley; t_B is the time measured by Betty, who remains safely on Earth; and v is the relative velocity of the two reference frames. Plugging in the numbers gives

$$t_A = 28\,[1-(0.9)^2]^{1/2}\ \text{years}$$

$$t_A = 28\,[1-.81]^{1/2}\ \text{years}$$

$$t_A = 12.2\ \text{years}$$

If Ashley turns around at her destination without stopping and heads back to Earth at the same speed, Betty will have aged 2 x 28 = 56 years, while the adventuresome Ashley will be only slightly more than 24 years older than when she started. That two people born on the same day could wind up with very different ages is not science fiction. It is real science. To reiterate, time is relative. It depends on one's frame of reference.

LENGTH CONTRACTION

Space is relative, too. Let us return to Ashley's trip. A careful examination reveals a problem. Ashley has covered 25 light-years in a little more than 12 years. Has Ashley has gone faster than the speed of light? No, of course not. Special relativity tells us that nothing can travel faster than light, a law that will be derived later. So, what's going on?

From Ashley's point of view, she traveled at 0.9c for 12 years. That is a distance of 0.9 x 12 light-years. So, Ashley measures the distance to her destination as 11 light-years; Betty measures it as 25. The difference between the two distances is called **length contraction**. Space, it turns out, like time, depends on one's frame of reference.

WHAT'S SPECIAL ABOUT RELATIVITY?

Einstein's paper on relativity was the last of his miracle-year block-busters (but not his last paper; that honor would go to a short note about the interchangeability of mass and energy that will be examined in the next chapter). He confined his relativity paper to the special case of reference frames moving in a straight line at constant velocity. Consequently, it is called the special theory of relativity. The general theory, which applies to all frames of reference, including those not in uniform motion, took Einstein 10 more years to work out. It took that long because it included an entirely new concept of gravity, which will be covered as we learn about general relativity.

Relativistic Fallout

T he special theory can both confuse and surprise people who are trying to understand it for the first time. What follows is a discussion that deals with both of these reactions to relativity. Let us begin with the confusion. Albert Einstein's relativistic equations that show how space and time are not fixed are reasonably straightforward. Mass, like space and time, is also not fixed. However, unlike the other two quantities, just how it changes in reference frames that are moving relative to one another is a bit tricky.

RELATIVISTIC MASS

To understand how mass changes with velocity, let us return to the equation governing length contraction. That equation was published before Einstein proposed relativity theory. The phenomenon is called the Lorentz-Fitzgerald contraction, named after the two scientists—George Francis Fitzgerald and Hendrik Lorentz—who, working independently, first proposed it.

$$L_A = L_B \left(1 - \frac{V^2}{c^2} \right)^{\!\!1/2}$$

Here, L_B is the length of an object as measured in the object's frame of reference; L_A is the length as measured by an observer in an inertial reference frame moving with respect to the object. The Lorentz-Fitzgerald contraction states that an object moving relative to an observer is shortened *in the direction of motion* by an amount predicted by the equation. The dimensions of the object in other directions are unchanged.

Applying the Lorentz-Fitzgerald contraction in a seemingly simple thought experiment led to a confusing result and to one of the first serious challenges to Einstein's theory of special relativity. It involved some old ideas about the unchanging nature of mass—and a cherished principle of physics.

What follows is one version of that thought experiment. Visualize a long, straight highway stretching through millions of miles of empty space. Next, paint a line down its center. Finally, imagine our travelers Ashley and Betty revving up identical spaceships at opposite ends of the road. The twins zoom down the highway toward one another at close to the speed of light. Ashley stays just to the right of the line, while Betty stays to the left (Figure 4.2).

Their two ships are cruising at identical speeds. When they collide, it is a glancing blow that bounces both of them away from the line. The question is, what do the twins see just after the collision?

Let us call the line down the middle of the highway the x-axis and a line perpendicular to it the y axis. After the collision, Ashley will see that Betty's ship has moved, let's say 328 feet (100 meters) from the center of the road in the y direction. Since the collision is symmetrical, Ashley must have moved the same distance away from the x-axis. Figure 4.2 shows the position of the spaceships one second after the collision. Now, as measured in Ashley's frame of reference, how fast is Betty's ship moving away?

Remember, the Lorentz-Fitzgerald contraction occurs only in the direction of motion, so when Betty says she has moved 328 feet (100 m) away from the center line in one second, Ashley will see no shortening in that direction and will agree on the 328 feet (100 m). However, because she is moving relative to Betty in the x direction, she will disagree on the elapsed time. She will say that Betty's clock runs slow and that her clock shows that more than one second has elapsed.

This means that the velocity of Betty's ship must be less than Ashley's. It took only one second for Ashley's ship to move 328 feet

(continues on page 54)

Lorentz-Fitzgerald Contraction

In 1889, the Irish physicist George Francis Fitzgerald proposed a radical explanation of why the Michelson-Morley experiment failed to detect the luminiferous ether. His explanation came at a time when he, like most scientists, firmly believed in the ether. Movement through the ether, Fitzgerald said, shortened the arm of Michelson's interferometer just enough to cancel the decrease in the speed of light caused by the ether wind. This length contraction took place along the line of motion and was almost impossible to detect because any meter stick used to measure it would contract, too.

Two years after Fitzgerald published his proposal, Hendrik Lorentz, a prominent Dutch physicist who was also a staunch believer in the ether, developed the idea further. The shortening of objects in motion relative to an observer became known as the Lorentz-Fitzgerald contraction. Lorentz also came up with a general method for transforming the space and time coordinates of events from one inertial frame of reference to another. The equations he derived to do this are called Lorentz transformations, and they proved useful to Einstein as he developed the special theory.

Lorentz's formulas for calculating time dilation and length contraction are identical to those Einstein developed for special relativity. Why, then, are Lorentz and Fitzgerald not considered to be the authors of the theory of special relativity? The answer lies in the two men's wrong interpretation of the Michelson-Morley experiment. According to Lorentz and Fitzgerald, the ether existed and the speed of light was constant relative to it. Einstein's bold leap forward was to ignore the ether and accept what Maxwell's equations were telling him: The speed of light is the same for every observer. It is this key conclusion that led Einstein to relativity—and kept Lorentz and Fitzgerald from discovering it themselves.

Nevertheless, Einstein knew he owed much to the two men's groundbreaking ideas and was quick to recognize them. In an after-dinner speech he delivered in California, Einstein credited "the ideas of Lorentz and Fitzgerald, out of which the Special Theory of Relativity developed."

Figure 4.1 Hendrik Lorentz helped develop the Lorentz-Fitzgerald contraction to explain the apparent absence of relative motion between light and the ether (a medium once assumed to permeate space).

(continued from page 51)

(100 m) from the center line, but from Ashley's frame of reference, it took Betty's ship longer to move the same distance. Consequently, the momentum of the two ships, their mass times velocity, is also different. Thus, the collision appears to violate a long-standing principle of physics: the conservation of momentum.

This law states that the total momentum of the spaceships must be the same before and after the collision. However, according to relativity theory, the total momentum after the collision is less than before the collision because time dilation in Ashley's frame slowed the velocity of Betty's ship. Of course, from Betty's reference frame the reverse holds true, and Ashley's ship is moving slower. So, regardless of which reference frame is chosen, momentum is not conserved.

Can the conservation of momentum be rescued? Of course it can—if Einstein is available. To solve the problem, he hypothesized that the mass of an object depends on its speed relative to the reference frame in which it is measured. Mass, he concluded, must increase with speed according to the familiar relativistic equation.

$$m_{rel} = \frac{m_{rest}}{\left(1 - \frac{v^2}{c^2}\right)^{1/2}}$$

In this equation, m_{rest} is the at-rest mass of an object; that is, its mass as measured in an inertial reference frame in which it is motionless; m_{rel} is its relativistic mass, which is the mass of an object moving in an inertial reference frame. As is the case with time and distance, until an object approaches the speed of light, relativistic effects on mass are negligible. At a speed of 621 miles per second (1,000 km s^{-1}), for instance, the mass of an approximately 1,000 kg (1.1-ton) object would increase by less than 1 gram (0.4 ounces).

Nevertheless, this adjustment to at-rest mass rescues the conservation of momentum. The principle holds true in this thought experiment—and in all actual experiments.

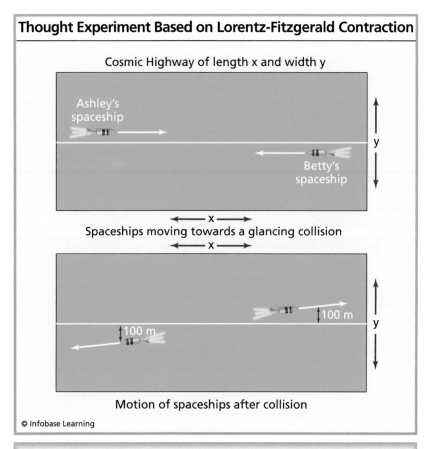

Thought Experiment Based on Lorentz-Fitzgerald Contraction

Cosmic Highway of length x and width y

Ashley's spaceship

y

Betty's spaceship

← x →

Spaceships moving towards a glancing collision

← x →

100 m

y

100 m

Motion of spaceships after collision

© Infobase Learning

Figure 4.2 Colliding space ships appeared to violate the conservation of momentum principle until Einstein showed how relativity affects the masses of moving objects

SPEED LIMIT

Two of the most surprising ideas in special relativity can be derived from the concept of relative mass. The first of these is the so-called **cosmic speed limit.** As mentioned earlier, relativity theory predicts that nothing can go faster than the speed of light in a vacuum. Does this speed limit make good sense? No, at least not in the nonrelativistic world. However, it is true as shown in a revealing thought experiment in which adventuresome Ashley attempts to exceed the cosmic speed limit.

She has traded in her old spaceship for a newer, bigger model; in fact, a much bigger one that is thousands of miles long. For ground transportation, she has brought along a very fast motorcycle that can reach speeds close to that of light. In deep space, Ashley's ship is cruising at a steady 0.8 times the speed of light or 0.8c. She then hops on her motorcycle in the rear of the ship and speeds it up to 0.7c (Figure 4.3). How fast is Ashley going?

The answer seems straightforward. If you are on a bus that is going 10 miles (16 km) per hour, and you get up and run toward the front door at 10 miles (16 km) per hour, then your speed relative to the ground is 10 + 10 = 20 miles (32 km) per hour. One just adds the two speeds, as Galileo himself told us.

Einstein, however, had a different idea. Using Lorentz transformations to relate the movement of bodies in different reference frames, he came up with a new equation for adding velocities. To calculate Ashley's speed on the motorcycle relative to Earth (or some other distant star), Einstein said, one must replace the old relationship

$$V = V_R + V_m$$

with

$$V = \frac{V_R + V_m}{1 + (V_R + V_m)}$$

In this equation, V_R is the velocity of the spaceship relative to Earth, V_m is the velocity of the motorcycle relative to the spaceship, and V is the velocity of the motorcycle relative to Earth. All velocities are expressed as a fraction of the speed of light. Now, one can calculate Ashley's speed on the motorcycle. The sum of the two velocities 0.8c + 0.7c = 1.5c is reduced by the relativistic factor in the denominator to give

$$V = \frac{0.8c + 0.7c}{1 + 0.56} = \frac{1.5c}{1.56} = 0.96c$$

No matter how fast Ashley drives her motorcycle, she will never exceed the speed of light. One cannot add velocities below the speed of light to reach the speed of light.

Relativistic Shortcuts

The common factor in the three equations that govern special relativity is

$$\frac{1}{\left(1 - \dfrac{V^2}{c^2}\right)^{\!1/2}}$$

It is convenient to give this factor its own symbol, the Greek letter gamma, δ. Using this notation, the equations can be restated as

Time dilation: $t = t_0 \delta$

Length contraction: $L = \dfrac{L_0}{\delta}$

Relativistic mass: $m = m_0 \delta$

In each case, the variable with subscript 0 represents the measurement made in the object's frame of reference.

This does not make much sense to a person running for the front door of the bus. How can your velocities add directly to give the correct answer of 20 miles (32 km) per hour? Surely, the relativistic calculation must be wrong. However, it is not. The equation that is wrong is the other one. Velocities do not add directly for anyone. We live in a relativistic world, but when the correct equation is used to determine the combined speeds of bus and passenger, it gives the same 20 miles (32 km) per hour. The reason, repeated here many times, is that until the relative velocities approach the speed of light, the laws of Galileo and Newton work just fine.

You may have noticed an assumption in the spaceship-motorcycle example. It takes as a given that the spaceship itself cannot go faster that the speed of light. Well, why not? The answer can be found in the concept of relativistic mass. These days, physicists prefer to use relativistic momentum to explain the cosmic speed

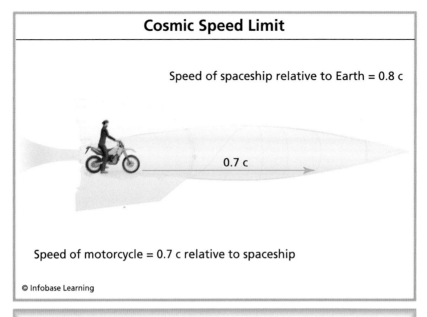

Cosmic Speed Limit

Speed of spaceship relative to Earth = 0.8 c

0.7 c

Speed of motorcycle = 0.7 c relative to spaceship

© Infobase Learning

Figure 4.3   Velocities do not add directly in the relativistic universe. No matter how fast Ashley rides the motorcycle, her speed cannot exceed c, the cosmic speed limit.

limit. However, the idea of relativistic mass is easier to follow, so it will be used here.

Let us return now to the equation for mass.

$$m_{rel} = \frac{m_{rest}}{\left(1 - \dfrac{V^2}{c^2}\right)^{1/2}}$$

The factor in the denominator

$$\left(1 - \frac{V^2}{c^2}\right)^{1/2}$$

gets smaller as V approaches c. Consequently, the mass of the object increases. However, according to Newton's second law of motion, $F = ma$, so the greater the mass, the greater the force required to accelerate it. At V = c, the object's mass is infinite, so the force required to accelerate it must also be infinite. Because there are no infinite forces, *V* can never reach *c*. The speed of light is an unbreakable limit.

THE MOST FAMOUS EQUATION

A few months after publishing his paper on special relativity, Einstein wrote to a friend: "One more consequence of the electrodynamics [special relativity] paper has also crossed my mind. Namely, the relativity principle, together with Maxwell's equations, requires that mass be a direct measure of the energy contained in a body." Einstein expanded on this idea in a short paper in September 1905, the third and last paper he wrote in his miracle year.

Using some simple algebra and some-not-so-simple physical reasoning, Einstein produced a form of the now famous equation

$$E = mc^2$$

Direct and simple as always, Einstein concluded his paper by saying: "The mass of a body is a measure of its energy content." This means that energy and mass are two forms of the same thing. This revelation was, and remains, a stunning and surprising result of the special theory of relativity.

MISCONCEPTIONS

Some people believe $E = mc^2$ led directly to the creation of the atomic bomb. It did not. It is true that Einstein's 1939 letter to President Franklin Roosevelt about the potential for using nuclear fission in bombs sparked the Manhattan Project, which led to the first atomic bomb. Einstein, however, had nothing to do with that effort. The idea for the letter that kicked off the project came from other scientists who wanted to use Einstein's prestige to get Roosevelt's attention.

Another misconception about the world's most famous equation is that it applies only to nuclear processes. In fact, all energy-generating operations convert mass to energy. Your car, for instance, burns gasoline to produce the energy that moves the car down the road. Where does the energy come from? The answer is $E = mc^2$. If you could weigh the gasoline in the tank very accurately and collect all of the material released during combustion, their weights would not be the same. The collected material would weigh less. Not much less, of course, but less. The missing matter was converted to energy, the energy that propelled your car.

Let's take this idea step further. Suppose your town uses coal to generate electric power while a neighboring town of the same size uses the same amount of energy in a year but gets it from a nuclear reactor. If all the coal your town burned in a year were weighed along with all the ashes and output gases, you would find that the weight of the residual materials was less than the weight of the coal. Furthermore, that loss in weight would be exactly equal to the weight loss of uranium in your neighbor's nuclear plant.

Of course, such measurements would be difficult to make because the mass consumed is small. A glance at Einstein's equation tells why. The multiplier of mass contains the speed of light. It is a very big number, and its square is an even bigger one. So, even a tiny bit of mass has the potential to generate a huge amount of energy. As Richard Wolfson points out in his book *Simply Einstein*, a single raisin—if converted completely to energy—could power all of New York City for a day. A small package could keep it going for months.

A dramatic example of the huge conversion factor relating mass to energy took place on August 6, 1945, when the world's first atomic bomb was dropped on Hiroshima, Japan. It completely destroyed the center of the city and damaged much of the rest. More than 100,000 people died from the blast and the resulting radiation poisoning. How much uranium had to be converted to energy to cause so much death and destruction? Less than 0.03 ounce (1 gram).

TIME TRAVEL: PART III

The reason that the twins' adventure in space travel is called a paradox has nothing to do with their different rates of aging. That is a straightforward result of special relativity. No, Ashley's trip to a distant planet is a paradox because of the conclusion reached centuries ago by Galileo. All motion, he said, was relative. If that is so, then Ashley's trip to a faraway planet could really be Betty's trip. Ashley hops into her spaceship and the Earth (and Betty) rockets away from her. This appears to be just as valid a way of looking at the twins' travel as the reverse. However, it is not.

Recall that Ashley had to accelerate when she left Earth to reach her cruising speed. She had to turn around when she arrived at her destination and had to decelerate when she got back to Earth. Meanwhile, Betty has stayed in an inertial frame the whole time. The twins have had entirely different experiences. The time they

Figure 4.4   Twisted metal and rubble fills what once was Japan's most industrialized city, Hiroshima, seen in 1945 after the atomic bomb was dropped.

spent in uniform motion accounts for the disparity in their ages, but it does not clear up the central problem presented in the paradox. The twins have had different experiences, yes, but why should Ashley be the lucky, younger one? From Ashley's perspective in the spaceship, Betty is zooming away. Why is it not Betty's clock that is running slow?

Quite a few mathematicians and physicists have attacked this problem by employing the methods of special relativity. Their conclusions as to why Ashley ends up younger than Betty can be found in math-heavy journal articles. However, a simpler route to ridding ourselves of this paradox is possible. When we revisit the twins in a later chapter, general relativity will provide a satisfying resolution.

IS ANY OF THIS TRUE?

According to special relativity, time dilates, space contracts, and mass changes with velocity. Special relativity leads to some outlandish conclusions, but it seems to make sense. As presented here, however, it has been constructed solely out of Einstein's reasoning and tested only in thought experiments. At this point, a skeptical reader should be asking whether any of is this true. Where is the experimental evidence?

Special relativity is true, and it is routinely used in modern gadgets. Older television sets would have been disconcertingly blurry if the paths of electrons were not corrected for their increase in mass as they travel toward the screen. The precision clocks used in Global Positioning Systems (GPS) would put users in the wrong place if they were not corrected for time dilation and other relativistic effects. Furthermore, the particle colliders that transform mass into energy would make no sense at all without $E = mc^2$.

The effects of special relativity have also been demonstrated in numerous experiments. However, one experiment—the **muon** experiment—stands out above the others for its clear confirmation of special relativity. Muons are highly energetic, short-lived, charged particles that form when cosmic rays encounter atoms and molecules in Earth's upper atmosphere. Some muons make it down to Earth's surface, but they do not hang around long. They have a **half-life** of only about 1.5 microseconds (1.5 X 10^{-6} s).

In the early 1960s, D.H. Frisch and J.H. Smith, two Massachusetts Institute of Technology (MIT) scientists, used the muon rain to measure the time dilation feature of special relativity. The experiment was a marvel of simplicity and accuracy.

Muons approach Earth at close to the speed of light. The two men set up a detector to count the muons with speeds between 0.9950c and 0.9954c. The first measurements were made at the top of Mount Washington, a 6,288-foot (1,917-m) mountain in New Hampshire. They found that an average of 563 muons within that speed range struck their detector in an hour. Knowing the half-life and speed of the muons, the experimenters then calculated the number that should reach sea level.

If relativistic effects are ignored, the number should drop off substantially due the muons' very short half-life. "What do we expect for the intensity at sea level?" the two scientists asked in their classic 1963 paper. The answer they came up with was about 27 muons per hour. They then made sea-level measurements using the same detector. They found that an average of 408 muons hit their detector in an hour, much higher than the expected number from the non-relativistic prediction.

Why the discrepancy? Relativity, of course. The time it takes for a muon to travel from the top of Mount Washington to sea level is easily determined. Simply divide the muon's velocity by the distance to get an answer of about 6.4 microseconds. That, of course, is the answer for an observer in Earth's frame of reference. However, what about the muons themselves? Their reference frame is just as valid as that of the scientists. How much time do they experience on that same trip? Remember, moving clocks run slow, and the muons are moving very fast.

Using Einstein's formula for time dilation, one can calculate the amount of time the muons experience on their journey. It comes to about 0.64 microseconds. From that, one can calculate the number of muons that should reach sea level when relativistic effects are considered. The rate here turns out to be 400 muons per hour,

Muon Rain Detection

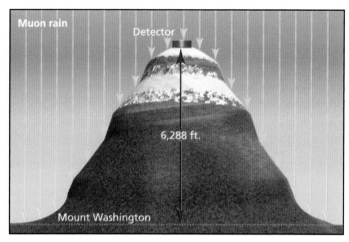

563 muons per hour strike detector

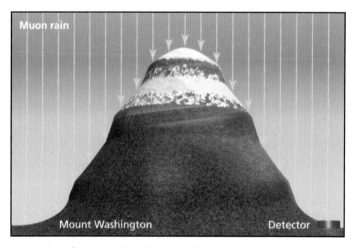

Expected number of muons striking detector with no correction for relativity = 27 per hour
Expected number after corrections for relativity = 400
Experimental result = 400 ± 9

© Infobase Learning

Figure 4.5 As portrayed in these illustrations, muon measurements confirm Albert Einstein's special theory of relativity.

which agrees closely with the experimental average of 408 ± 9. This experiment shows as clearly as possible that special relativity is not just a neat theory. It is how the world works.

That last statement, however, is not altogether correct. Special relativity predicts how that part of the world contained in inertial reference frames works. The next chapter will explore what happens in reference frames that are accelerating. This requires Einstein's most mind-boggling creation: the general theory of relativity.

5

The General Theory of Relativity

Albert Einstein's theory of special relativity beautifully accounts for the dynamics of objects in frames of reference in uniform motion. With that success behind him, Einstein was ready to extend the theory to reference frames in accelerated motion. He realized that the problem with special relativity lies in the sneaky term *uniform motion*. How do you know when you are in uniform motion? Usually, it is an easy question. If you are in a car in nonuniform motion, turning a corner or accelerating, you will feel it. You will be thrown to the side or pressed into the car seat. When an airplane is in nonuniform motion caused by turbulent weather, drinks get spilled and pretzels fly all over. Things that are easy to do in uniformly moving reference frames, such as juggling, are almost impossible in nonuniform frames. However, Einstein came up with a clever thought experiment in which uniform and nonuniform reference frames are indistinguishable.

EQUIVALENCE PRINCIPLE

Supposing our space traveler Ashley is enclosed in a windowless room in outer space where gravitational effects are vanishingly small. What would happen if that room was accelerated upward at a rate of 32.1 feet (9.8 m) per second? That is the same rate of acceleration

Principle of Equivalence

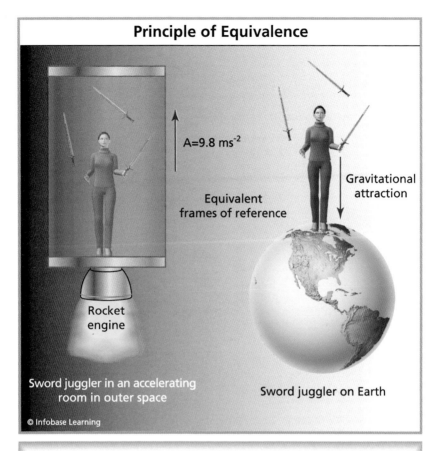

$A=9.8 \text{ ms}^{-2}$

Equivalent
frames of reference

Gravitational
attraction

Rocket
engine

Sword juggler in an accelerating
room in outer space

Sword juggler on Earth

© Infobase Learning

Figure 5.1   Gravity is equivalent in every way to an accelerating reference frame.

that one experiences on the surface of Earth, the acceleration due to gravity. Although Ashley is in deep space, far from any source of gravity, she would feel her feet pressed to the floor just as if she were standing on Earth.

Furthermore, if Ashley took a quarter from her pocket and dropped it, the coin would fall to the floor just as it would in Earth's gravitational field. In fact, she could juggle swords if she chose to— or perform physics experiments. The results would be the same as if she were standing on Earth.

Is there any way for people in an enclosed room to tell whether they are in Earth's gravitational field or in an accelerating reference

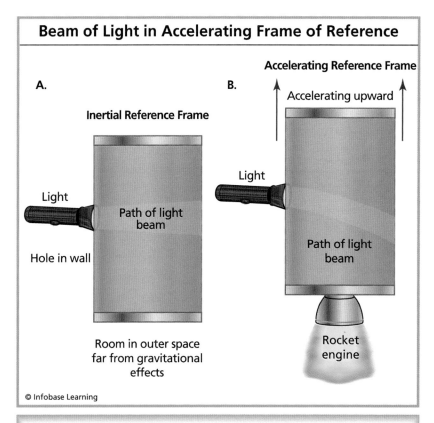

Beam of Light in Accelerating Frame of Reference

A.

Inertial Reference Frame

Light

Path of light beam

Hole in wall

Room in outer space far from gravitational effects

B.

Accelerating Reference Frame

Accelerating upward

Light

Path of light beam

Rocket engine

© Infobase Learning

Figure 5.2 This illustration shows how an accelerating reference frame, which is equivalent to gravity, bends light.

frame? The answer, Einstein concluded, is no. Gravity is equivalent in every way to an accelerating reference frame. Einstein conceived this **equivalence principle** two years after publishing his special theory in 1905, and it became a cornerstone of general relativity.

One consequence of the principle, Einstein realized, was its effect on light. When a flashlight is shined through a small hole in a windowless room, the beam goes straight across. Now, attach a rocket to the room and ignite it. As it accelerates upward, the beam of light would enter the same hole but by the time it crossed the room, the room itself would have moved upward. The result? The light would strike the opposite wall at a point closer to the floor (Figure 5.2B).

The beam of light in the accelerating reference frame is no longer straight. It is bent. However, the equivalence principle states that an accelerating reference frame is indistinguishable from a gravitational field. Thus, Einstein reasoned, gravity must bend light. Einstein would later use this startling conclusion to propose an experiment that would make him famous—and confirm the general theory of relativity.

WHAT IS GRAVITY?

All of us have a deep intuitive sense of gravity. When you lean too far over, you fall; when you run uphill, you pant. The first person to develop a quantitative understanding of gravity was Isaac Newton. It is not clear how he came up with his law of universal gravitation. There is, of course, the story about young Newton sitting beneath an apple tree and wondering if the force that pulled the apple to the earth was the same force that held the Moon in its orbit.

The story is probably apocryphal. Newton himself said that he discovered the secrets of gravity "by thinking of them without ceasing." That version seems to fit what we know about his workaholic habits better than the inspiration of the falling apple. Newton's law of gravity states that every object in the universe is attracted to every other object. The force of attraction between any two of them is proportional to the masses of the objects and inversely proportional to the square of the distance separating them. As mentioned earlier, this statement can be summarized as the equation,

$$F\alpha\frac{m_1m_2}{d^2}$$

Or, as it is more commonly written,

$$F=\frac{Gm_1m_2}{d^2}$$

where G is the gravitational constant, which has the same value everywhere in the universe.

The first person to identify a problem with Newton's law was Newton himself. How can the Sun, which never touches Earth, hold the planet in orbit? How can it reach out across 93 million miles (150 million km) of empty space and affect the trajectory of Earth? As mentioned earlier, this action-at-a-distance property of gravity disturbed Newton. He was unable to account for it and refused to theorize about it: As he so memorably put it, "I do not feign hypotheses."

More than two centuries would pass before someone did "feign hypotheses." That person was, of course, Albert Einstein. His general theory of relativity supplanted the Newtonian concepts of space, time, and gravity. Although Newton's famous inverse-square formula still works well for most applications, it fails in extreme conditions. Einstein's approach has never failed.

A MORE GENERAL THEORY

After the equivalence principle, the next big step toward the general theory came from Einstein's former math professor, Hermann Minkowski. Minkowski was amazed that Einstein could come up with a scientific idea as elegant as the special theory. "It came as a tremendous surprise," he told another physicist, "for in his student days Einstein had been a lazy dog."

The special theory showed that time and space are relative. The time between two events depends on the reference frame in which it is measured. So, too, does the distance (or space) between events. How then could one specify when and where an event occurred?

To answer the question, Minkowski introduced a new concept, **space-time** or, as it is sometimes called, Minkowski space. By specifying the coordinates of an event in four-dimensional space-time, one could pinpoint where and when it took place. Three of these coordinates are the ordinary dimensions of space (x,y,z). The fourth is time. One needs all four coordinates (x,y,z,t) to pin down an event.

Space-time is impossible for most of us to visualize. The mathematics are also difficult to master. However, the concept itself is simple enough. Minkowski himself summarized it somewhat

Figure 5.3   By 1907 Hermann Minkowski realized that the theory of special relativity, introduced by Albert Einstein two years earlier, could be best understood in a four-dimensional space in which time and space are intermingled in four-dimensional space-time.

dramatically: "Henceforth space by itself, and time by itself, are doomed to fade away into mere shadows, and only a union of the two will preserve an independent reality." Minkowski's insight was helpful to Einstein as he went about the grueling work of extending the special theory of relativity to reference frames not in uniform motion.

The principle of equivalence that linked accelerating frames of reference to gravity was firmly in Einstein's mind. Einstein also accepted that gravity (and therefore mass) bent light. Furthermore, Minkowski's work had showed that four-dimensional space-time was required to specify events. However, Einstein needed to develop the mathematics to describe how matter in a gravitational field affects the geometry of four-dimensional space-time.

In 1912, he began to work on this problem. For centuries, the only geometry available came from the Greek mathematician Euclid, whose textbook on the subject, *Elements*, is still the best-selling mathematics text ever written. Euclidian geometry is the geometry taught in high school. It tells us that parallel lines never intersect, and that the sum of the angles in a triangle is always 180°. Unfortunately, almost all of these good, common-sense rules do not hold in four-dimensional space-time. That left Einstein with a problem.

The equivalence principle told him that light followed a curved path in a gravitational field. Maybe, he speculated, space-time itself was curved. He needed a new geometry, one that described a curved, four-dimensional space.

Fortunately, such a geometry existed. A friend introduced Einstein to the geometry of curved multidimensional spaces that was developed more than 50 years earlier by the German mathematician Bernhard Riemann. After much work, Einstein mastered the difficult math he needed.

So, where did gravity fit in this four-dimensional curved universe? In a truly great leap of imagination, Einstein "realized that the foundations of geometry have physical significance." In other words, gravity *is* curved space-time. Bending light beams are not really bending at all, they are following a straight line in curved space-time. What causes space-time to curve? Here, Einstein and Newton agree: Mass is responsible for gravity. However, the two scientists' concepts of how gravity operates are entirely different.

Newton said that gravity is an attractive force that reaches across space. However, Einstein concluded that mass curves space-time in a manner that causes a body to move with no forces acting on it. In a gravitational field, the curvature of space-time will move you toward a massive object without any applied force at all; or, to put it differently, the geometry of space-time expresses itself as the force we call gravity.

These are difficult ideas to get your mind around. The mathematics are difficult, too. However, Einstein's complicated math can be boiled down to a single concise and elegant mathematical description of space-time.

$$R_{\mu\nu} - \tfrac{1}{2} R\, g_{\mu\nu} = 8\,\pi\, G\, T_{\mu\nu}$$

One can extract the essence of this equation without worrying about the precise meaning of the symbols, some of which are complex mathematical entities called **tensors**. As written, the left side of the equation describes the curved geometry of space-time. The right-hand side specifies how matter moves in space-time.

Einstein took general relativity public in a series of four lectures in November 1915. It had taken him 10 years to extend the special theory. The long delay should surprise no one. The concepts and mathematics behind the general theory are revolutionary, subtle, and difficult. The theory completely recast the way scientists regard the physical world. It was, according to the quantum mechanics pioneer and Nobel laureate Paul Dirac, "probably the greatest scientific discovery ever made."

One reason the general theory is so difficult to grasp is because few, if any, of us can visualize a curved four-dimensional space with time as one of the coordinates. Possibly the simplest and best way of summarizing how gravity works in a relativistic universe came from the physicist John Archibald Wheeler: "Matter tells space-time how to curve, and curved space tells matter how to move."

Although there is no good way to visualize how matter curves four-dimensional space-time, a two-dimensional analogy can help. Consider a bowling ball resting in the middle of a trampoline (Figure 5.4). If you roll a marble onto the trampoline, it will follow a curved path around the massive bowling ball. No force is acting on the marble, it is simply following the path of least resistance. The marble's trajectory depends on the degree to which the bowling ball warps the

More About Tensors

There is no way to make the mathematics of general relativity easy. Einstein's equation looks simple, but it is not. The reason it appears to be straightforward and compact is Einstein's use of tensors.

Tensors are useful in physics because, as one textbook puts it, "the notion of a vector is too restricted" to handle some physical problems. Students have stated this idea more memorably, if less accurately: Tensors are vectors on steroids.

Exactly what are tensors? Here is the definition from a mathematics dictionary: "tensor, n. a multilinear differential form invariant with respect to a group of permissible coordinate transformations in *n*-space." A simpler explanation is that tensors express a relationship among vectors. Some tensors can be expressed as a matrix in which the elements are vectors.

Tensors come in several flavors. Einstein's equation for general relativity, for instance, contains three different types. One, the so-called **metric tensor** $g_{\mu\nu}$, was the key that allowed Einstein to account for the curvature of space-time due to the presence of the gravitational field.

In general relativity, these tensors disguise a very complicated and difficult set of equations. For example, each of the two subscripts of g in Einstein's equation stands for the four coordinates of space-time. Thus, the tensor notation is a compact representation of $4 \times 4 = 16$ equations. Fortunately, some of these are redundant, so there are actually only 10 equations. Unfortunately, they are some of the toughest equations in physics to solve. That is why Newton's formula for calculating gravitational forces is preferred for most applications, even though it is less accurate than general relativity.

trampoline as well as the speed of the marble. Slow marbles will follow a curved path around the bowling ball before falling off the trampoline. In the absence of friction, faster moving ones will go into orbit.

Bowling Ball on Trampoline Analogy

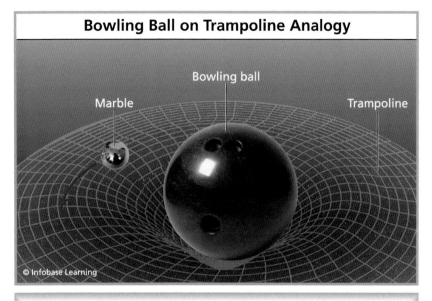

Figure 5.4   This two-dimensional representation is analogous to the rotation of Earth around the Sun in curved space-time.

The bowling ball-trampoline analogy, while useful, can be misleading. A force is required to start the marble moving on the trampoline, but in a gravitational field in space-time, no forces are involved.

CONCLUSION

To many of us, general relativity theory seems farfetched. Gravity is no longer a force acting between bodies but the result of the geometry of curved space-time. Although we have presented strong evidence supporting the special theory, we've yet to offer a single experimental result to substantiate the general theory. However, the theory has already answered the big question about gravity that stumped Newton himself. How does the Sun, which never touches Earth, hold it in orbit? According to relativity, the answer is that Earth is traveling a straight line in a region of space-time that is curved by the presence of the Sun. This eliminates the action-at-a-distance problem that troubled Newton.

6

Making the Case

In 1913, two years before his final, triumphant lectures on general relativity, Albert Einstein thought he had completed his work. "I finally solved the problem a few weeks ago," he wrote in a letter to Elsa Einstein, his cousin and wife-to-be. "It is a bold extension of the theory of relativity. . . ."

A month after publishing the paper, Einstein was having second thoughts about his work. The equations were not as general as he wanted, and they did not hold for all reference frames. Nevertheless, Einstein was confident enough to test the theory. He was aware of a problem that Newtonian physics could not explain: a tiny discrepancy in the orbit of Mercury.

THE PROBLEM WITH MERCURY

In a simple system of one planet orbiting a much larger body such as a star, the laws of German mathematician Johannes Kepler and Newton state that the planet should trace out an elliptical orbit around the star. The point of the planet's closest approach to the star is a fixed point called the **perihelion**.

Of course, real planets—those in our Solar System, for instance—do not follow this script exactly. Their perihelions are not fixed. They move, or precess, around the Sun (Figure 6.1). These deviations from a simple, one-planet system are due mainly to the presence of the

Advance of Perihelion

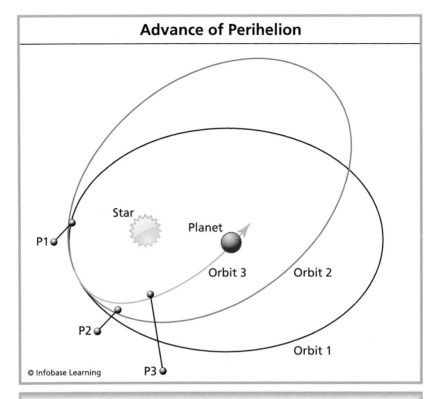

Figure 6.1   The advance of perihelion, in which a planet orbits a star, is shown. The theory of relativity predicts that, as it orbits the Sun, Mercury does not exactly retrace the same path each time, but rather swings around over time. Therefore, the perihelion—the point in Mercury's orbit when it is closest to the Sun—advances.

other planets whose gravitational fields perturb each other's orbits. Using Newton's laws, one can account for the precession of the perihelions of all of the planets—except Mercury.

Even after taking into account the effect of gravity from all known sources, Mercury obstinately refuses to obey Newton's laws. The difference between the observed precession of its perihelion and the one calculated using Newton's formulas was small, only 43 **arcseconds** per century. This is a tiny deviation. (One second of arc is only 1/3,600 of a degree.) However, the astronomers' measurements were so accurate, that they were certain their observations were at odds with the Newtonian prediction.

One of the first scientists to tackle this puzzle was Jean Joseph Le Verrier, a French astronomer who had solved a similar problem, a discrepancy in the orbit of Uranus. Le Verrier had predicted that an undiscovered planet caused Uranus's erratic course. Shortly afterward, the new planet—Neptune—was spotted by astronomers.

Fresh from that success, Le Verrier turned to Mercury. He applied the same logic that explained the deviant orbit of Uranus. The orbit of Mercury, he announced in 1860, was being perturbed by the presence of a never-seen planet, later named Vulcan. Several astronomers reported sighting it, but none of the sightings were ever confirmed.

By the beginning of the twentieth century, few astronomers believed that Vulcan existed, but they still could not explain Mercury's orbit. Einstein hoped relativity would provide the solution. Using the equations published in his 1913 paper, he calculated the rate of precession of Mercury's perihelion. The result was disappointing. The theory could only account for 18 arc-seconds per century of the 43 arc-second deviation from the laws of Newton.

A DISAPPOINTING YEAR

Disappointed but not defeated, Einstein turned to another test to make the case for relativity. The general theory predicts that gravity bends light. Einstein reached this conclusion in 1911 and proposed a test to determine if it was true. He calculated that the Sun would bend starlight passing near it and encouraged astronomers to measure the deflection.

Obtaining those measurements was difficult. The Sun is so bright that the stars cannot be seen except during a solar eclipse. The next solar eclipse was expected to take place on August 21, 1914. Einstein pushed for an expedition to the Crimea in Russia to make the necessary measurements. Unfortunately for Einstein (and many others), Germany declared war on Russia a few weeks before the eclipse was to occur, making travel impossible.

The failure of his theory to correctly predict the orbit of Mercury and the delay in testing the light-bending feature of relativity discouraged Einstein. Furthermore, his marriage to his first wife, Mileva, was in shambles and breaking up. In October 1915, things got even worse when Einstein finally faced up to a problem that had nagged him for two years. The equations published in 1913 were wrong. The laws of gravity predicted by his equations were not the same in all reference frames. This violated the central tenet of general relativity, that the laws of physics are the same everywhere.

SUCCESS FINALLY

This depressing turn of events spurred Einstein to greater efforts. He entered into a four-week frenzy of work. The result was a revised set of equations. Before making them public, he decided to apply the new equations to the problem of Mercury.

After a month of grueling work, after numerous false starts and disappointments, Einstein was ready to test his theory again. Could his revised general theory of relativity account for an astronomical fact that Newton's laws could not? On November 18, 1915, he used the new equations to calculate the precession of Mercury's perihelion. The answer agreed almost exactly with the observations of centuries of astronomers. The 43 arc-second per century deviation was gone. The prediction of relativity theory matched the observational evidence perfectly.

Einstein was elated. "I was beside myself with joyous excitement," he said. Abraham Pais, his colleague and biographer, knew Einstein's feelings about the matter as well as anyone. "This discovery was, I believe, by far the strongest emotional experience in Einstein's scientific life, perhaps in all his life," he wrote.

Einstein was aware that his general theory was much more than an ordinary scientific breakthrough. He had rewritten the fundamental laws of physics. None of this, however, made Einstein the household name he would soon become. That would take another calculation and another observation.

BENDING LIGHT

If you shout at people in the next room, they will hear you. However, if you shine a flashlight at them, they will not see it. Sound waves go around corners, but light waves do not. This fact, among others, led

Isaac Newton to conclude that light was not a wave but consisted of a stream of particles he called "corpuscles."

Corpuscles, Newton believed, were small bits of matter, and because they were matter, they should be affected by gravity. This led him to an important speculation: "Do not Bodies act upon Light at a distance, and by their action bend its Rays, and is not this action . . . strongest at the least distance?"

German physicist Johann Georg von Soldner investigated Newton's idea about the bending of light by gravity and published his findings in 1804. (Henry Cavendish, the English scientist who provided the experimental data needed to determine Newton's gravitational constant, made a similar calculation earlier but never published it.)

To make their calculations, both von Soldner and Cavendish assumed that light was composed of corpuscles of tiny, but unknown mass. Einstein was unaware of this work. However, when he began his own calculations, he knew that light corpuscles (or photons, as they would be named later) were massless. However, general relativity predicts that mass warps the fabric of space-time, so light waves traveling in a straight line through curved space-time would appear to be curved.

Einstein was well aware that objects under the influence of gravity accelerate at the same rate, regardless of their mass. Galileo had demonstrated this centuries earlier when he dropped a cannonball and a musket ball from a tower and saw that they hit the ground at the same time. So, Einstein did not need to know the effective mass of a photon to determine how much the Sun should deflect it. Employing classical Newtonian physics, he came up with an approximate formula for calculating the deflection of starlight by the Sun:

$$A = \frac{2Gm_2}{dc^2}$$

Here, A is the angle of deflection, G is the gravitational constant, m_2 is the mass of the Sun, and d is the closest distance between the incoming starlight and the Sun's center of gravity. As usual, c is the speed of light in a vacuum.

Plugging in the numbers, Einstein found that in a Newtonian world, the Sun should deflect the starlight grazing its surface by

0.9 arc-seconds. (Although Einstein did not know it, this was the same number that von Soldner had come up with more than 100 years earlier.) The calculated deflection is small. Nevertheless, it was measurable with the telescopes available at the time.

Keep in mind that the calculation for the Newtonian bending of light is problematic at best. We do not live in a Newtonian universe, and just how much gravity might bend light in that universe (if at all) is unknown. Still, Einstein's calculation is what astronomers in the early twentieth century used as the Newtonian prediction for the deflection of light. That was the angle to which the prediction of general relativity would be compared.

Einstein's theory predicted twice as much deflection as Newton's corpuscular theory. Like the precession of Mercury, the difference between the predictions was small but measurable. To make the measurements, though, four conditions had to be met: World War I had to end to make travel safe; a multitude of background stars must be located behind the Sun to ensure that rays of light from the stars would graze its surface; a clear sky was required to photograph the stars' apparent positions; and, of course, one had to have a solar eclipse.

It was almost four years after Einstein's "joyous excitement" over his correct prediction of Mercury's orbit before astronomers had a chance to make the measurements Einstein wanted. That occasion was the solar eclipse expected on May 29, 1919.

The person most interested in testing relativity theory was the English astronomer Arthur Stanley Eddington, who had been impressed by Einstein's work. The May eclipse offered an exceptional opportunity to make the measurements because the Sun would be in front of an unusually bright group of stars. During the eclipse, many of those stars would become visible. Their apparent positions could be photographed and compared to control photos showing their actual positions.

Plans to observe the eclipse were formalized after the armistice of 1918 ended the war. Two expeditions were mounted. Eddington led the one going to Principe, an island off the west coast of Africa. The other one headed for Brazil. Both teams had difficulties with their delicate telescopes and cameras. When the big day arrived, Principe was cloudy and rainy. Eddington managed to get only two usable photographs. The other team's main telescope worked poorly in the Amazonian heat and returned blurry photos. Only a smaller backup scope gave usable results.

After returning to England, Eddington checked and double-checked the results. His team came up with a deflection of 1.61 arc-seconds. The Brazil expedition measured 1.98 arc-seconds. Einstein's predicted value of 1.74 arc-seconds was well within the 95% confidence range of both sets of measurements, while the Newtonian prediction of 0.87 arc-seconds was not. The general theory of relativity—first tested on the orbit of Mercury—was confirmed.

Einstein took the news calmly. "I knew the theory was correct," he told a graduate student on the day the results arrived in Germany. He might have been (or pretended to be) nonchalant, but the rest of the war-weary world was looking for something to celebrate. Headlines everywhere trumpeted the news: "New Theory of the Universe, Newtonian Ideas Overthrown," blared the *Times* of London. The *New York Times* followed with "Einstein Theory Triumphs." Einstein became a celebrity of the first order, as recognizable as any movie star.

The fame was deserved. Einstein's theory did not just explain new data but also gave scientists a whole new way of looking at the physical world. So far, his theory had accounted for only a few minor discrepancies in Newtonian physics. However, the general theory would later be used to probe the secrets of the universe.

One example of such probing is how astronomers exploit the bending of light predicted by general relativity in order to see deep into space.

EINSTEIN'S TELESCOPE

Even before he finished working out the final equations of general relativity, Einstein postulated that a star or galaxy could act as a magnifying lens. This was not a far-fetched idea. Ordinary optical lenses bend light, just as gravity does. So, Einstein reasoned, it should be possible to use gravity as a lens.

Of course, the physics behind the two types of lenses is entirely different. Optical lenses depend on refraction, the change in direction of an electromagnetic wave when it passes from one substance to another—air to glass, for example. Gravitational lensing occurs when

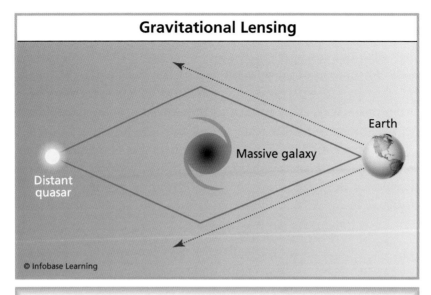

Gravitational Lensing

Earth

Massive galaxy

Distant quasar

© Infobase Learning

Figure 6.2   In this example of gravitational lensing, a massive galaxy lies between Earth and a quasar, a bright, distant, celestial body. The dashed lines show two directions the light can take to reach Earth. The result can be two distinct images.

two massive bodies (or groups of bodies)—stars, galaxies, galaxy clusters—line up relative to Earth. Light from the more distant source curves around the nearer one (Figure 6.2). The light is following a straight line in curved space. The curve is due to the warping of space-time by the massive object(s) between Earth and the distant stars.

Unlike optical lenses, which can be machined and assembled to order, with gravitational lenses observers have to take whatever nature gives. Although astronomers speculated for years about the possibilities of gravitational lenses, they were unable to locate one. The object that enabled them to finally find one was an astronomical curiosity called the **quasar**, or quasi-stellar object.

Quasars are the most energetic bodies in the universe. They are associated with the super massive **black holes** that lie in the center of many galaxies. Billions of years ago, when the universe was younger, these black holes were eating everything around them and emitting enormous amounts of electromagnetic radiation. The more luminous ones are brighter than a trillion Suns. Astronomers today can see quasars that lie halfway across the universe.

In 1979, astronomers sighted a rarity, a double quasar. Both quasars were about 6 billion light-years from Earth. Astronomers knew they were quasars because no stars would be visible from that far away. An analysis of the quasars' spectra showed them to be identical. Two quasars with exactly the same spectra are about as likely as two humans with exactly the same fingerprints. It simply could not be. Astronomers quickly realized that they were looking through a gravitational lens that was producing two images of the same thing.

Gravitational lenses can do strange things. The images one sees depend on the exact alignment and distances of the bodies. For instance, in Figure 6.2, the observer sees two images of the same

Gravitational Lens G2237+0305

Figure 6.3   The four points in this Hubble Space Telescope photograph of Einstein's Cross are part of a single, distant quasar.

body, but one might see four images as the light curves around the lensing body.

A spectacular example of quadruple imaging is the Einstein Cross. The cross is actually four images of one quasar located about 8 billion light-years from Earth. The object in the center of the photograph is the lens, a galaxy about 400 million light-years away.

The Einstein Cross is a relatively simple example of gravitational lensing. Most images are not that easy to interpret. One complicating factor is **dark matter,** which is matter whose presence can only be inferred from its gravitational effect on stars and galaxies. Because these lenses are artifacts of gravity, the presence of dark matter affects how they work. The combination of ordinary and dark matter can produce bewildering and distorted images. However, under the proper conditions of location, distance, and alignment, gravitational lenses can do exactly what optical lenses do—produce clear, magnified images of distant objects. Using gravity in this creative way enables astronomers to peer deeper into the universe and has earned these lenses their own name: "Einstein's telescopes."

WHERE ARE YOU?

How do you know where you are? More and more people rely on information from the Global Positioning System (GPS). The heart of the system is a network of 24 to 36 satellites in orbit around the Earth.

Although most of us think of GPS receivers as personal assistants—handheld devices, or gadgets built in the dashboard of a car—they are used in many other ways. Airlines, space shuttles, and search-and-rescue missions all depend on GPS. So do mapmakers and astronomers and people in many other professions. Modern society is not yet completely dependent on GPS, but it is moving in that direction.

One reason why GPS systems are so widely available today is due to a tragedy. In 1983, Korean Airlines Flight 007 strayed into the Soviet Union's restricted airspace. It was shot down by fighter planes, killing all 269 passengers and crew. To help avoid future navigational disasters, President Ronald Reagan issued an order to make GPS available to everyone in the United States when its development was complete. The first satellite was launched in 1989, and the system was fully operational in 1995.

Trilateration

Pretend you are lost somewhere on Earth. You may not know it, but your GPS receiver will use trilateration to figure out where you are.

It works like this: Your receiver detects a signal from a satellite and calculates that it is x meters away. Now where are you? Well, you still do not know for sure, but you can narrow your position down. All the points on Earth that are x meters from the satellite lie on the circumference of a circle (Figure 6.4A). (This example assumes that Earth is a smooth, perfect sphere.)

Now, your receiver picks up another signal from another satellite. Just as before, your receiver figures out the distance to the satellite, enabling you to draw another circle. You now have considerably more information about your location. In fact, because only two points on Earth are equidistant from both satellites, you have narrowed your position down to just two possibilities, the points shown where the circles intersect (Figure 6.4B).

Finally, your receiver picks up the signal from a third satellite. The result is that the point where all three circles intersect is where you are (see Figure 6.4C).

If your receiver detects signals from additional satellites, it can nail down your position more precisely. Of course, this analysis does not give you the receiver's altitude. That requires more complicated mathematics and the signals from a fourth satellite.

(opposite) Figure 6.4 In simple GPS trilateration, the points are determined by measuring distances, using the geometry of circles or spheres.

GPS relies on a process called trilateration, which involves knowing the distances between satellites and receivers. The distance is calculated by measuring the time it takes for a signal from a

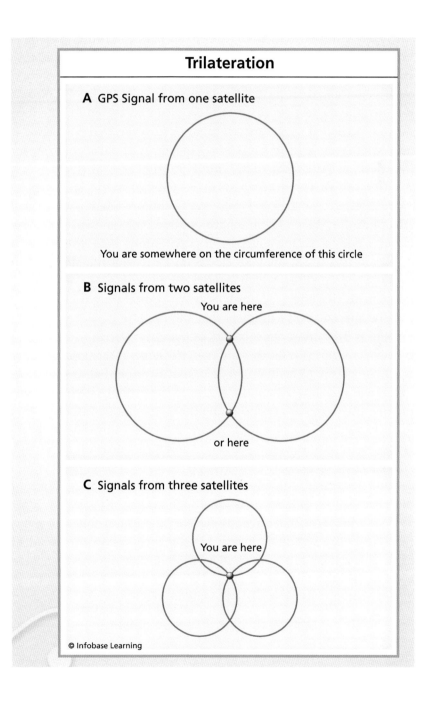

Trilateration

A GPS Signal from one satellite

You are somewhere on the circumference of this circle

B Signals from two satellites

You are here

or here

C Signals from three satellites

You are here

© Infobase Learning

satellite to reach a receiver on Earth. By measuring the times of signals from several satellites, usually four of them, at different distances from the receiver, the device can calculate its position. To ensure the correct time, each satellite carries a super-accurate atomic clock. Some very clever mathematics enables these atomic clocks to adjust the less-accurate clocks in the receivers. It is a well-designed, very useful system, and it would not work at all without Albert Einstein's contribution.

As mentioned earlier, the time measurements used in GPS would not give the correct results if they were not corrected for the time dilation predicted by the special theory. However, that correction is only half the story. In fact, it is less than half. Without accounting for the effects of *general* relativity, your GPS would be worthless.

This should come as no surprise. Gravity is the geometry of space-time. A gravitational field warps that geometry, which will affect not only space (as in length contraction) but also time. The closer a body is to the source of a gravitational field, the slower a clock will run. Thus, the GPS clocks on Earth will run slower than those in the satellites, which are ticking away in a weaker gravitational field. This effect is known as **gravitational time dilation**.

The special theory predicts that the satellite clocks, which are moving at 2.42 miles per second (3,895 m s^{-1}) relative to Earth, run slower than those on Earth. However, the general theory states that clocks in a strong gravitational field, that is those that are closer to Earth, will run slower than the clocks in the distant satellites. Thus, the two effects tend to cancel each other out—but not exactly.

The satellite clocks will tick more slowly than the Earth-bound clocks by 7.2 microseconds per day. (A microsecond is usually abbreviated as μs.) However, due to general relativity, the super-accurate cesium clocks in the satellites tick faster by about 45.9 μs. Without the relativistic correction, the clocks would be off by 45.9 − 7.2 = 38.7 μs every day. This might appear to be a minor difference, but remember, the system is measuring distances using the speed of light. This is a big multiplier and a tiny error in time creates a large error in distance. The speed of light is roughly 300,000,000 m s^{-1}, so during that 38.7-μs interval, light would travel

$$(38.7 \times 10^{-6})(3 \times 10^{8}) = 11{,}600 \text{ m}$$

This is a huge error, and one that would grow with time. Without Einstein's correction, GPS would be of little value. However, when it is corrected for relativistic effects, it is a very useful tool, enabling users to pinpoint their position to less than 10 m (33 feet).

CONCLUSION

The theory of relativity, both special and general, has been tested over and over again. It has passed every test with flying colors. Furthermore, predictions derived from the theories have helped make modern life possible in developments from nuclear power to GPS. However, one of the predictions of general relativity is so bizarre that it was ignored for years. The next chapter will deal with that prediction. Solutions to Einstein's equations indicate that the curvature of space can become so extreme that nothing—not even light—can escape. The result is the strange object mentioned earlier—a black hole.

7

Black Holes

It is unfortunate, but not uncommon, that brilliant, farseeing scientists sometimes produce theories that are so far ahead of their time that they are ignored. Ancient Greek philosopher Democritus, for instance, proposed an atomic theory about 400 B.C. Yet his idea about atoms languished until English scientist John Dalton came along with a more complete version about 2,200 years later. A similar fate befell English scientist John Michell, who proposed in 1783 that bodies whose "light could not arrive at us" could exist. Today, such bodies are called black holes.

Michell's ideas were based on Newtonian physics, the only physics available at the time. First, like Newton, he assumed that light was made up of corpuscles. Second, because corpuscles were matter, he—like von Soldner and Cavendish—expected they would be affected by gravity. Michell's ideas about the existence of black holes are worth exploring because Newtonian physics provides a good introduction to them. Later, we will use Einstein's more accurate, but more difficult, theory to examine them further. What follows is a modernized version of Michell's thinking.

BLACK HOLES: NEWTON

Toss a baseball straight up over your head. Its initial acceleration as it leaves your hand will temporarily overcome gravity. However, as

Figure 7.1 In 1783, John Michell published a visionary paper in which he predicted the existence of bodies so dense that not even light could escape their gravitational pull. Today, such bodies are called black holes.

the force of gravity tugs downward on the ball, it slows, stops, and returns to Earth. (Remember, this example is presented in Newtonian language; relatively speaking, gravity is not a force at all but the curvature of space-time). Throw harder and the ball will rise higher. Throw very hard, and the ball will overcome Earth's gravity, sail into space, and never return.

The minimum speed you have to throw the ball for it to leave Earth (or any other massive body) permanently is called the **escape speed**, the formula for which is

$$V_{esc} = \left(\frac{2Gm}{d} \right)^{\frac{1}{2}}$$

In this equation, G is the gravitational constant, m is the mass of the Earth, and d is the distance between the thrown ball and Earth's center. Notice that escape speed is independent of the mass of the departing object. It is the same for a rocket ship as it is for a baseball.

Plugging in the numbers for an object leaving the surface of the Earth, one gets an escape speed of 25,000 miles per hour (11,200 m s^{-1}). On the Moon, the getaway speed is less than 5,000 miles per hour (2,235 m s^{-1}). To permanently leave the Sun, a much more massive body, one must speed up to well over a million miles per hour or 447,000 m s^{-1}.

Now, what happens if d, the distance to a body's center of gravity, gets smaller? In that case, if its mass stays the same, its density will increase as will the speed required to overcome its gravity.

To return to the earlier example, one would have to throw the baseball harder to overcome gravity if the Earth was compressed to a smaller size. Finally, if Earth were compressed enough, the speed that the ball would have to reach to overcome gravity and permanently escape into space would equal the speed of light. In this case, special relativity states that nothing can exceed the speed of light, so nothing could ever leave the compressed Earth. Furthermore, because no light can escape, such a body would be perfectly black: a black hole.

Michell's Newtonian approach is a simplified, but useful, way of thinking about black holes. However, by the time Einstein came along, Michell's ideas had been forgotten. However, general relativity provided a new tool for exploring the possibility of black holes. Surprisingly, the man whose work would lead to their discovery was not Einstein himself, but another German scientist whose work complemented Einstein's.

BLACK HOLES: EINSTEIN AND SCHWARZSCHILD

Just weeks after Einstein published his general theory of relativity in 1915, he received a letter. It began, "Verehrter Herr [Dear Mr.] Einstein!" The writer of the note provided some calculations that he hoped would make Einstein's theory "shine with increased purity." The laudatory letter was written by Karl Schwarzschild, a distinguished astronomer and physicist. Included in it were the first exact solutions to Einstein's relativity equations. (Einstein had used an approximation to come up with his prediction about the perihelion of Mercury.)

Einstein was impressed. "I would not have expected that the exact solution to the problem could be formulated so simply," he wrote back. Schwarzschild's work was remarkable for three reasons: First, the speed with which he grasped Einstein's theory was amazing; second, the mathematical ingenuity he displayed in exactly solving the equations of general relativity was equally amazing; finally, and even more amazingly, when Schwarzschild wrote his letter, he was not working in a quiet, comfortable office, but serving as an officer in the German army in the chaos of the Russian front during World War I.

The war going on around Schwarzschild did not stop this remarkable man from applying Einstein's equations to a real-world problem: How does a star affect space-time? To simplify the mathematics, Schwarzschild assumed the star was spherical and not spinning. His solution showed how the curvature of space-time becomes more pronounced the nearer one approaches a star.

His next paper showed what happens to space-time *inside* a star. Those results contained a bombshell. Taken to the extreme, Schwarzschild's geometry made a startling prediction with which many scientists (including Einstein himself) could not agree: It implied that any object, if sufficiently compressed, will become a black hole.

Figure 7.2   In 1916, Karl Schwarzschild—photographed here in 1905—introduced the idea that when a star contracts under gravity, there will come a point at which the gravitational field is so intense that nothing, not even light, can escape. The radius to which a star of a given mass must contract to reach this stage is known as the Schwarzschild radius. Stars that have contracted below this are known as black holes.

Schwarzschild had little time to contemplate this staggering possibility. Weeks after writing his papers, he contracted a rare skin disease called pemphigus, in which the autoimmune system attacks the skin cells. The result is painful, disfiguring blisters for which there was no remedy. He died on May 11, 1916, less than six months after he responded to Einstein's paper.

Einstein himself read Schwarzschild's obituary to a meeting of the Prussian Academy. About a year later, a longer one was published in *The Astrophysical Journal* by Schwarzschild's colleague Ejnar Hertzsprung. "We have reached the height of life," Schwarzschild told the writer shortly before his death, "Before long we shall go downward." Schwarzschild, Hertzsprung wrote, "did not live to see that time." He died "at the summit of productivity. . . . He died standing." It was a fitting epitaph for a determined, competent scientist.

Although Schwarzschild was gone, his contributions to science were not. Within a few years, his space-time geometry was being used by physicists to explore the nature of stars. Every star has a critical size, astronomers concluded, which is now called its **Schwarzschild radius**. If a star (or any other body) is compressed beyond that size, its mass would warp space-time so severely that light could not escape, thus forming a black hole.

In theory, then, black holes are easy to make. All one has to do is shrink a body below its Schwarzschild radius. The Schwarzschild radius, r_s, for any object of mass m is

$$r_s = \frac{2Gm}{c^2}$$

where G is the gravitational constant and c is the speed of light in a vacuum. The equation makes it clear that an object's Schwarzschild radius depends only on its mass. Upon rearranging the equation, one gets

$$c = \left(\frac{2Gm}{r_s} \right)^{1/2}$$

This is the same relationship given earlier for escape speed. Its meaning is clear. At an object's Schwarzschild radius, its escape speed is equal to the speed of light. Because nothing can exceed the speed of light, nothing can escape the gravitational grasp of such an object. This leads to the definition of a black hole as any object smaller than its Schwarzschild radius.

HOW TO MAKE A BLACK HOLE

By the 1930s, some scientists (but not Einstein) believed that black holes might exist, but no one knew how they could be created because of the extremely high pressures that are required. One would have to squeeze the Sun down from its current radius of about 435,000 miles (700,000 km) to 1.9 miles (3 km). To make a black hole out of the Earth, it would have to be compressed to the size of a pea. The question facing physicists was, could anything generate such high pressures? Furthermore, if so, what? The answers—yes and gravity—were found in the stars.

Stars are a balance between the inward pull of gravity and the outward pressure exerted by the hot gases in the interior. The energy that heats the gases comes from nuclear fusion. However, the fuel for that fusion, mainly hydrogen and helium, will eventually be exhausted, and when it is gone, gravity is there waiting. Under its relentless force, the star collapses.

The endpoint of a star's collapse depends on its size. Stars with mass about the same as the Sun go through several stages as they die, expanding and contracting and blowing off outer layers of gas as they deplete their nuclear fuel. What is finally left is the smoldering core of the gravitationally compressed star, a dense remnant of carbon and oxygen ions and electrons. The pressure that pushes back against further collapse is not the pressure of a hot gas as it is in a shining star. It comes from the **Pauli exclusion principle**.

The increasing gravitational pressure in the remnant core squeezes the electrons together, forming an electron **degenerate gas**. Because, as Pauli's famous principle states, no two electrons not clearly separated by position can occupy the same quantum state, further compression pushes them into higher and higher energy levels. These high-energy, high-speed electrons strongly resist compression. This resistance to compression is called the electron degeneracy pressure. It is present in all matter, but it is negligibly small at ordinary densities.

When stars the size of the Sun collapse, the degeneracy pressure counterbalances the force of gravity. The result is a dense object

Star Mass and Size

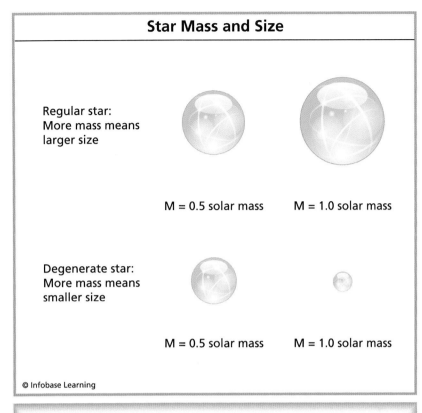

Regular star:
More mass means
larger size

M = 0.5 solar mass   M = 1.0 solar mass

Degenerate star:
More mass means
smaller size

M = 0.5 solar mass   M = 1.0 solar mass

© Infobase Learning

Figure 7.3   Unlike ordinary stars, the size of white dwarfs *decrease* with increasing mass.

called a **white dwarf**. These remnant stars are a consequence of extreme gravity, which has left them with extraordinary properties.

A star the size of the Sun will wind up as a white dwarf about the size of Earth. The density of a typical white dwarf is 10^9 kilograms per cubic meter, one million times the density of water. A single teaspoon of white dwarf would weigh more than 5 tons (4,536 kg).

Another curious property of degenerate matter is the relationship between size and mass. Double the mass of a normal star or an ordinary gas (or liquid or solid) at a fixed pressure and temperature and its volume will double. Double the mass of a white dwarf and its volume will *decrease*. This means that a larger star will form a smaller white dwarf.

The culprit behind this surprising property is gravity: More mass means higher gravity. Higher gravity produces higher density—and smaller size.

In some cases, gravity can overcome the pressure of the electron degenerate gas that is resisting it. This occurs when the remnant star is significantly more massive than the Sun. This divide between ordinary white dwarfs and those that undergo further compression is called the **Chandrasekhar limit**. It is named for the Indian physicist Subrahmanyan Chandrasekhar who proposed it in 1935.

Chandrasekhar showed that electron degeneracy pressure could not balance the crush of gravity if the mass of a white dwarf exceeded 1.4 times the mass of the Sun. At the time, he did not speculate on what would happen to such a star, except that it would continue to collapse. It was only later that scientists determined the fate of star remnants with masses exceeding the Chandrasekhar limit.

NOVAS

Every now and then, new stars pop up in the sky only to fade away over time. They were called **novas** by early sky watchers. Novas have been sighted throughout history. The Danish astronomer Tycho Brahe saw one in 1572. It was, he wrote, "the greatest wonder that has ever showed itself in the whole of nature . . ." Thirty-two years later, Johannes Kepler, his former employee, spotted another one.

Until the twentieth century, no one knew how far away the new stars were, so no one knew how bright they were. In the 1920s, Edwin Hubble figured out a way to measure the distances to other galaxies. Novas turned out to be much farther away than most astronomers had believed. That meant that the novas were much brighter than previously thought. Astronomers soon discovered that there were two main types of novas, one much brighter than the other. The astrophysicist Fritz Zwicky called these super-novas. Shortly afterward the hyphen was dropped and the term *supernova* entered the language.

Supernovas are not functioning stars but those going through explosive death throes. These are the most violent happenings in the universe. Over a period of a few days or weeks, a supernova will generate enough energy to outshine an entire galaxy containing billions of stars. This is the fate of dying stars with masses higher than the Chandrasekhar limit.

Supernovas are complex events that fall into two categories. (For our purposes, the several subdivisions of these categories can be ignored.) Type I supernovas typically occur when a white dwarf sucks enough matter from another star to push it above the Chandrasekhar limit. This results in a runaway thermonuclear explosion, usually leading to the complete disintegration of the star.

Type II supernovas are caused by the gravitational collapse of large stars that have exhausted their fuel supply. Much of the star is blasted off into space, but a remnant is often left behind. If the mass of the remnant exceeds the Chandrasekhar limit, it collapses further. Electrons are squeezed into protons to form neutrons. The gravitational collapse may finally be halted by the pressure of the remnant's neutron degenerate gas. The result is an astounding object called a **neutron star**.

A neutron star has a density approaching that of an atomic nucleus. The packed-together neutrons make a white dwarf look downright fluffy. A typical neutron star packs an entire Sun into a sphere about 6.2 miles (10 km) in diameter. This gives it an average density of about 10^{17} kg per cubic meter, about 100,000,000 times as dense as a white dwarf. One teaspoon of this stuff would weigh 500 million tons (454 billion kg).

The super-high density produces *extreme* gravity. If one could stand on a neutron star (which, of course you cannot as you would be immediately squashed flat) and drop a baseball, it would be going about 2,000 km s^{-1} when it hit the ground. In other words, gravity has accelerated the baseball from a standstill to more than 4 million miles per hour (6.4 million km per hour) in a 3.2-foot (1 m) drop.

One can trot out other astounding statistics about neutron stars: their rate of rotation for instance—very fast; their temperature— very high. However, what is even more astounding is what happens when even more massive stars collapse. If a supernova blast leaves a remnant larger than three solar masses, even a neutron degenerate gas cannot withstand the force of gravity. The star collapses further, forming a black hole.

Nonrotating black holes have a spherical boundary, a surface of no return called the **event horizon**, which has a radius equal to the object's Schwarzschild radius. Anything passing the event horizon is forever lost to the outside world.

Slimming Down Black Holes

Once past the event horizon, nothing can escape from a black hole. This means that black holes can never get smaller. They are destined to always grow larger. This was the conventional thinking until 1974 when the British physicist Stephen Hawking, who once held Isaac Newton's old post of Lucasian Professor of Mathematics at Cambridge University, figured out how a black hole might slim down.

The improbable idea of a shrinking black hole begins with the equally improbable idea that a perfect vacuum is not really empty. In fact, it seethes with so-called **virtual particles**. Virtual particles are particles which flash into and out of existence spontaneously. Here is how Hawking explains it: "What we think of as 'empty' space cannot be completely empty because that would mean that all the fields, such as the gravitational and electromagnetic fields, would have to be exactly zero." However, the **uncertainty principle** tells us that the fields in empty space cannot be fixed at zero. "There must be a certain minimum amount of uncertainty, or quantum fluctuations, in the value of the

One way to understand black holes is to imagine what would happen to a person—you, for instance—as you approach the event horizon of a large black hole. Falling freely into the void, you would feel nothing different. Your watch would run normally, and you would not even know when you sailed past the event horizon. Once inside, you would be pulled toward the black hole's center. Soon, you would begin to feel a differential pull as the curvature of space became significant relative to the size of your body. Then, you would be ripped to pieces.

Of course, all of this is speculation. Although scientists are reasonably sure about what goes on inside a black hole, no one has ever been inside one and returned to tell about it. Also, because black holes are so different from ordinary matter, some of their features are difficult to pin down. For example, black holes form when matter collapses, but how far can matter collapse and where does it go? Or, to put it another way, what lies in the center of a black hole?

field," he concludes. These fluctuations manifest themselves as virtual particles.

Virtual particles always come in pairs. A virtual electron, for instance, is always paired with a virtual positron. However, energy cannot be created out of nothing, so the total energy of the virtual particle pair must be zero. If one particle has positive energy, then the other must have an equal amount of negative energy. Normally, after a very short life, the two particles recombine and annihilate one another.

However, if a virtual particle pair forms near the event horizon of a black hole, then the particle with negative energy could fall into the black hole while the one with positive energy escapes. To an observer, the black hole appears to be emitting particles with positive energy. These emissions are known as Hawking radiation. Furthermore, according to Einstein's famous equation, the negative energy of the infalling particle is equivalent to a negative mass, so the mass of the black hole must decrease.

In a human being, this process would amount to losing weight by taking negative calorie pills, an invention that has yet to happen—but will be a big money maker if it does.

With nothing capable of stopping its gravitational collapse, the mass of a black hole shrinks to an infinitely dense point. Such a point is called a **singularity**. A simple example of a mathematical singularity is dividing by zero. What is $1/x$ when $x = 0$? No one knows, so therefore, it is undefined. The same thing happens at the singularity of a black hole. Infinitely dense matter creates infinitely curved space-time. The result is the end point of extreme gravity—an undefined, chaotic, dimensionless point.

DO BLACK HOLES EXIST?

Since Michell's day, many of science's top theorists have speculated about the nature of black holes. Einstein doubted they existed. Chandrasekhar believed they did. In addition to these two physicists, many other distinguished scientists—among them, J. Robert Oppenheimer, who led the Manhattan Project during World War II, and John Wheeler, who coined the term "black hole"—weighed in with their ideas, calculations, and theories.

Until recently, observational astronomers could add little to this debate. After all, black holes are invisible. It was not until the beginning of space-based astronomy that hands-on astronomers began to contribute. The launching of detectors above Earth's atmosphere opened a new window for watching the heavens. One surprise was the discovery that X-rays—which cannot penetrate Earth's atmosphere—were flashing through the universe.

Most of these X-ray emissions came from **binary stars**. Binary stars are not uncommon. They usually consist of two ordinary stars orbiting a common center of mass. If the two stars are close together, gas can flow from one to the other. Binary systems of this sort emit radiation in the visible range. However, a special class of binary stars emits very high energy X-rays. If the gravitational pull of the attracting body is strong, the infalling gas is heated to temperatures so high that X-rays are given off. The only bodies with sufficient gravity to accelerate a gas to those speeds are very dense objects—white dwarfs, neutron stars, and black holes.

The first X-ray binary star was discovered in 1964. It was a strong X-ray emitter named Cygnus X-1, located about 6,000 light-years away. Scientists suspected that the source of the high-energy emissions might be matter being sucked into a black hole. This star was the subject of a friendly wager between two prominent investigators of black holes: Stephen Hawking and Kip Thorne, a professor of theoretical physics at the California Institute of Technology.

Thorne held that Cygnus X-1 was a black hole; Hawking disagreed. They made the bet in 1974. By 1990, Hawking had conceded: Cygnus X-1 was almost certainly a black hole. The evidence came from tracking the motion of the normal star in the binary system. Its orbit indicated that the unseen body it is locked into contained about 8.7 solar masses. That was far too massive for it to be a white dwarf or neutron star. The only other possibility was a black hole.

Research on the X-ray emissions of binary stars was aided by the 1999 launch of the Chandra X-ray Observatory, appropriately named for Subrahmanyan Chandrasekhar. Using Chandra and a battery of new instruments, many other likely black holes have been

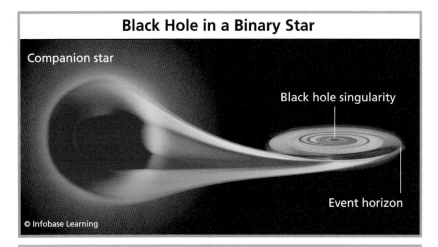

Figure 7.4   This is an artist's depiction of a black hole in a binary system sucking gas away from its companion star, producing X-rays. Eventually, all that will be left is a bigger black hole.

identified and classified by size. The observatory has also generated spectroscopic data that allows scientists to piece together the details of how a black hole functions in a binary star (Figure 7.4).

SUMMING UP

Although general relativity is conceptually and mathematically difficult, it is correct and useful. Among other things, it successfully predicts the properties of black holes. The next chapter will use general relativity to wrap up the story of the space-traveling twins Ashley and Betty. It will also show how Einstein spent the last years of his life in a gallant, but unsuccessful, attempt to marry relativity to electromagnetic field theory and quantum mechanics.

8

The Twins, Relativity, and Beyond

No aspect of relativity fascinates the public as much as the twins paradox. It is completely counterintuitive. How could two people born at the same time wind up with different ages? In addition, it is not only the public that is beguiled by the paradox. Scientists are still fussing over it, too. Papers attempting to explain the twins' age divergence continue to appear. Most of these explanations are based on special relativity. Some of them are long and complicated. Some are disputed by other scientists. Fortunately, there is a simple way to clear up the paradox.

GENERAL RELATIVITY AND THE TWIN PARADOX

Special relativity accounts for the twins' age difference. Moving clocks do indeed run slow, as was conclusively shown in the muon experiment (and others). The question posed by the paradox is: Which twin is moving? If all motion is relative, as Galileo said, then why could stay-at-home Betty not be the twin moving away from adventurous Ashley's spaceship? In which case, Betty's clock would run slower and she would be the younger when the two were reunited.

It is clear that the twins had different experiences. Ashley underwent acceleration on her trip, while Betty did not. However, why should that lead to Ashley winding up as the younger twin?

To resolve the paradox, recall the gravitational time-dilation effect that had to be corrected for in GPS. General relativity predicts that strong gravitational fields cause clocks to tick slower. Furthermore, the equivalence principle states that gravity and acceleration are indistinguishable. Therefore, the acceleration Ashley experienced in her spaceship was equivalent to placing her in a gravitational field. Therefore, it is her clock that must run slower. She must be the younger twin. Paradox solved.

AFTER RELATIVITY

Celebrity scientists are rare. Newton was one and so was Benjamin Franklin. More recently, Carl Sagan, Stephen Hawking, and Richard Feynman made it into this realm. Still, no other scientist in the twentieth century even came close to Einstein's celebrity. After the 1919 eclipse and Eddington's data showing that the Sun bends starlight as predicted by general relativity, Einstein became a scientific superstar. "It doesn't take an Einstein," became a common phrase when discussing easy-to-solve problems.

Einstein earned his celebrity. The years he struggled with the general theory were hard on him and his family. However, during that time, he never wavered from the goal of condensing and simplifying the complexities of space-time into a concise mathematical statement. "It can scarcely be denied," he said in a lecture he delivered at Oxford University, "that the supreme goal of all theory is to make the irreducible basic elements as simple and as few as possible without having to surrender the adequate representation of a single datum of experience." This statement is commonly shortened to "Everything should be made as simple as possible, but no simpler."

This is not a farfetched notion in science. Most scientists believe that the best theory is the one that explains the greatest number of observations with the fewest axioms. It is clear that Einstein was a strong believer in this principle. During the last three decades of his life, he would doggedly pursue the goal of simplifying physics by attempting to unite relativity theory with electromagnetism and, later, with quantum theory. This goal he would call the **unified field theory**.

Before beginning his quest for the unified field theory, Einstein collected a few major awards. Chief among them was the 1921 Nobel

Occam's Razor

Occam's Razor is referred to today as "KISS": "Keep it simple, stupid." The meaning behind the phrase stretches back to William of Ockham (and possibly even before him). William was a Franciscan friar and philosopher who was born in the village of Ockham, about 25 miles (40 km) southwest of London. His date of birth is uncertain, but it was about 1280. It is also uncertain how "Ockham" (the village) became "Occam" (when it used in reference to "razor"), but eventually it did, at least in most references.

Writing in 1320, William made a famous pronouncement. "Entities," he wrote, "should not be multiplied unnecessarily." Scientists love this idea, and many of them, including Isaac Newton, have rephrased it to suit themselves: "We are to admit no more causes of natural things than such as are both true and sufficient to explain their appearances." Nature, Newton concluded, prefers simplicity.

The razor in Occam's Razor was added to the principle in the nineteenth century. It implies that one should carve away the dead wood until one finds the simplest hypothesis that fits all the data. Another interpretation holds that the razor cuts through superfluous arguments to reach the correct one.

Occam's Razor is not a law of physics, and KISS is no substitute for the scientific method. However, when faced with competing hypotheses that make the same prediction, the simpler one is preferred. Over the years, many scientists (including Einstein) have concluded that applying Occam's Razor can be a shortcut to selecting the correct hypothesis, thus saving time and energy.

Prize in physics. He did not win for his work with relativity but for his explanation of the photoelectric effect, which showed that under some conditions light, which had long been considered to be a wave, could act as a particle.

Einstein's 1921 Nobel actually came a year late, in 1922. The committee could not agree at first on who should get the 1921 prize for physics, so none was given. However, in the following year, two awards were handed out. The 1921 prize went to Einstein; Niels Bohr received the 1922 award for his contributions to quantum mechanics. Both awards were well deserved, recognizing the achievements of two of the most important scientists of the twentieth century.

Einstein, a maverick as usual, focused his Nobel lecture not on the work that won the prize but on relativity. He also spoke about the research he intended to pursue in the future. As usual, he thought big. "We seek a mathematically unified field theory," he told his audience, "in which the gravitational field and the electromagnetic field are interpreted only as different components or manifestations of the same uniform field."

Soon afterward, he expanded this goal to encompass a problem that had nagged him for years. His work on the photoelectric effect had been a huge leap forward in the quantum theory. However, Einstein detested the recent direction that quantum mechanics had taken. The new quantum theory, proposed and promoted by Niels Bohr and his group in Copenhagen, was based on statistics, probabilities, and uncertainty. Einstein summed up his feelings about it in a famous one-liner. "I am convinced," he wrote in a letter to another physicist, "that He [God] does not throw dice. One can't make a theory out of a lot of 'maybes.'" A unified field theory, Einstein thought, would not only unite relativity with electromagnetism but also with quantum mechanics. It would smooth out the discontinuities and eliminate the uncertainties associated with the theory.

Einstein would pursue the goal of a unified field theory for the rest of his life. By the 1920s, he was such a celebrity that his progress was heralded in newspapers. "Einstein Reduces All Physics to One Law," was one *New York Times* headline in 1929. Of course, the headline was wrong, as the breakthrough proved to be a blind alley. Undaunted, Einstein continued working, publishing papers on a unified field theory, then finding flaws and retracting them.

TOWARD THE END

Einstein's contributions to science declined after his work on relativity, but he continued to travel, receive awards, and lecture widely. Although he would never replicate the glory days of his early discoveries, he did continue to do solid scientific research. For instance, he played a major role in developing **Bose-Einstein statistics**, which predicted the existence of a new form of matter.

When small amounts of some substances are cooled almost to absolute zero, Bose-Einstein statistics predict that all of the atoms will lock into the same quantum configuration. This makes them useful tools for scientists studying quantum mechanics. By observing the substance—now called the **Bose-Einstein condensate**—they can actually *see* quantum effects. Einstein and a young physicist in India named Satyendra Nath Bose predicted the existence of the condensate in 1924, but it took some time before someone actually produced one. When a sample was finally available for study in the lab, its properties were identical to those the two physicists had predicted 70 years earlier.

The story behind this discovery tells a great deal about Einstein as a person. It started with a letter from Bose, who enclosed an unpublished paper that intrigued Einstein. It featured a creative twist in the statistical analysis of the quantum states of photons. Bose, who was a complete unknown in scientific circles, could not get any journal to accept his paper.

Einstein used his sway to get it published in a prestigious scientific journal. He then followed up with three additional articles that extended Bose's idea from photons to atoms. This led to the prediction of the Bose-Einstein condensate. Later, when Bose's lack of a Ph.D. prevented him from getting a university position, Einstein used his influence to help him get one.

This spirit of generosity and a willingness to give credit to other scientists for their contributions was typical of Einstein. He was warmhearted toward collaborators and colleagues and, for a superstar, unusually modest about his own work.

After the rise of the Nazis in 1932 forced him to flee Germany, Einstein moved to the United States. He accepted a position at the newly formed Institute for Advanced Study in Princeton, New Jersey. It was there that Einstein found his final home. He had a good

Figure 8.1 Satyendra Nath Bose is best known for his work in quantum statistics. In 1924, Albert Einstein helped Bose get an important paper published and extended Bose's theories to create a general statistics of quantum systems. This is known as Bose-Einstein statistics and deals with particles with an integral spin. These particles are now called bosons.

salary and no other duties. He continued to pursue a unified field theory but harbored no illusions about the way he was regarded by other scientists.

In his book *The One True Platonic Heaven*, author John Casti imagines a fictional conversation between Einstein and the distinguished logician Kurt Gödel, who was also a faculty member at the institute. In this excerpt, Einstein is explaining his situation at the institute to Gödel. Although these are Casti's words, not Einstein's, the passage likely mirrors Einstein's sentiments at the time:

> When I came to the Institute in 1933, Mr. Flexner [founder and first director of the institute] made it perfectly clear by his actions that he had bought me for the Institute and that my role here was to be a ceremonial figurehead, an icon, if you like. Now I am afraid the faculty thinks of me as a bit of a dinosaur. They tolerate my ideas more from respect for my past work than from enthusiasm for my current ideas. . . .

THE END

In his ten-year struggle to complete general relativity, Einstein proved that he was a determined scientist. He demonstrated the same stubbornness in his work on a unified field theory. He ran into dead end after dead end, but he never gave up. At age 75, he was still wrestling daily with the equations he hoped would produce a new theory, one that was simpler, more beautiful, and more encompassing than those that preceded it.

A year later, Einstein collapsed with a ruptured aneurysm. Doctors recommended surgery. Einstein refused. "It is tasteless to prolong life artificially," he told them. "I have done my share; it is time to go. I will do it elegantly." Albert Einstein died on April 18, 1955, at the age of 76. Beside his deathbed was the last thing he wrote: 12 pages of equations that he hoped would unify science—a unified field theory.

EINSTEIN'S LEGACY

Einstein loved to talk physics, and he collaborated with many scientists. One of his biographers, Abraham Pais, listed 28 men and women with whom he worked closely. However, all of Einstein's big papers—the most important ones—were published without coauthors.

The range of his insights was staggering. Einstein played the starring role in twentieth-century science. His work affected almost every aspect of physics, from the quantum theory of atoms to the geometry of the universe. His work could have easily justified three Nobel Prizes—and that would be just for the papers he published in his miracle year of 1905.

However, most physicists would agree that Einstein's greatest contribution came ten years later in 1915 with the publication of his paper on general relativity. That theory reshaped our concept of the universe. Some historians believe that other scientists were close to developing the special theory of relativity—but not the general theory. It ranks with Maxwell's laws of electromagnetism and Newton's laws of motion and gravity in importance, and is in a class all by itself in conceptual difficulty. To paraphrase English theoretical physicist Paul A.M. Dirac's assessment, the general theory of relativity might be the greatest scientific discovery ever made.

Glossary

arc-second   An angular measure equal to 1/3600 of a degree

binary star   A pair of stars revolving around a common center of mass

black hole   An object so dense that nothing, including light, can escape its gravity

Bose-Einstein condensate   An exotic state of matter with zero viscosity that forms at very low temperatures when bosons condense to create a superfluid

Bose-Einstein statistics   Statistics that describe the distribution of energy states of certain types of particles (bosons) that do not obey the Pauli Exclusion Principle

Brownian motion   The motion of microscopic particles suspended in a fluid; Einstein showed that their movement was a result of collisions between the particles and the molecules of the medium in which they are suspended.

Chandrasekhar limit   The limiting mass of a white dwarf; any nonrotating white dwarf with a mass exceeding the Chandrasekhar limit of 1.4 solar masses will undergo further gravitational collapse to become a neutron star or black hole.

cosmic speed limit   The speed of light in a vacuum

dark matter   Matter whose presence is inferred from its gravitational effect on stars and galaxies; dark matter has not yet been directly detected.

degenerate gas   A highly dense form of matter that resists further compression because of quantum effects

electric field   A region in which an electrically charged particle experiences a force, usually due to the presence of other charged particles

equivalence principle   The key insight that led Einstein to general relativity; it states that gravity and accelerated motion are indistinguishable.

escape speed   The minimum speed that an object must reach to permanently overcome the gravitational attraction of another object

event horizon   The surface of no return of a black hole; at the event horizon, escape speed equals the speed of light.

frame of reference   A framework in which all objects are participating in the same motion; special relativity predicts that time and distance depend on the frame of reference in which they are measured.

general relativity   Einstein's theory that describes how mass curves space-time and how that curvature manifests itself as gravity

gravitational field   The region of space around a body with mass

gravitational time dilation   A prediction of general relativity that says that clocks in a strong gravitational field run slower than those in a weaker one; this effect has been experimentally confirmed.

half-life   The time it takes for half of any given amount of matter to undergo radioactive decay

inertial reference frame   A frame in which objects move in a straight line at constant speed unless acted upon by an external force

length contraction (also called the Lorentz-Fitzgerald contraction)   A consequence of the special theory of relativity that predicts that the length of an object in a reference frame moving relative to an observer appears contracted in the direction of motion; the length is a maximum in the frame in which the object is at rest.

light-year   The distance light travels in a vacuum in one year, about 9.5×10^{15} meters

luminiferous ether   The hypothetical medium through which light was supposed to propagate; the Michelson-Morley experiment of 1887 was unable to detect its existence.

magnetic field   A region in which magnetic materials experience a force, due to the presence of other magnets or moving electric charges; the field at any given point is specified by a force with direction and magnitude.

metric tensor   A mathematical construct used to determine the distance between points in multidimensional spaces; it is an essential element in Einstein's equation for general relativity.

muon (also known as the μ-meson)   A subatomic particle with a very short half-life; muons are detected on Earth when cosmic rays collide with atoms and molecules in the upper atmosphere.

nova   A star that dramatically increases in brightness due to a cataclysmic event, then slowly fades away

neutron star   The super-dense remnant of an exploding star; neutron stars are prevented from collapsing further to form black holes by the pressure of neutron degenerate gas.

Occam's Razor   A rule of thumb which states that when faced with competing hypotheses, one should choose the simplest one that fits all the data

partial derivative   The derivative of a function with two or more variables with respect to one of the variables when the others are held constant

Pauli exclusion principle   Principle that states that no two identical fermions in a quantum system can possess an identical set of quantum numbers

perihelion   The point in the solar orbit of a planet (or satellite or comet) where it is nearest the Sun

photoelectric effect   The ejection of electrons from a metal by electromagnetic radiation; Einstein investigated this effect and concluded that light was quantized and came in energy packets called photons.

photon   A particle with energy but no mass; it represents a quantum of electromagnetic radiation.

quanta   The plural of quantum; the minimum energy required to change certain properties such as the energy of an electron in an atom.

quantum theory   The theory first advanced by Max Planck which posited that energy was not continuous but came in small, discrete packages called quanta

quasar   Extraordinarily energetic sources of radiation believed to be emitted by hot gases being sucked into a black hole; the name is a contraction of "quasi-stellar" objects.

Schwarzschild radius   The radius of the event horizon of a black hole; any object compressed to its Schwarzschild radius becomes a black hole.

singularity   A point at which a mathematical function is not defined; every black hole is believed to contain a singularity of infinite density.

space-time   The combination of three-dimensional space with time; all four coordinates are required to specify an event.

special relativity   Einstein's theory that the laws of physics are the same in all inertial reference frames; the general theory extended this principle to all reference frames.

supernova   An exploding star that is temporarily brighter than all the stars in a galaxy

tensors   Mathematical entities that express relationships between vectors

time dilation   This special theory states that the time between two events is not absolute but depends on the reference frame in which it is measured

uncertainty principle   The principle, proposed by Werner Heisenberg in 1927, which states that it is impossible to know exactly both the postion and momentum of a particle

unified field theory   A comprehensive, but unfinished, theory that originally aimed to unite general relativity and electromagnetic theory; Einstein later expanded the goal to include quantum theory.

universal gravitation law   Newton's law that expresses the force of attraction between all bodies possessing mass

vector   A quantity that specifies both magnitude and direction; force and velocity are vector quantities; time and temperature are not.

vector calculus   The branch of mathematics concerned with differentiation and integration of vectors; Maxwell's equations are expressed in the mathematics of vector calculus.

virtual particles   Short-lived particle pairs that can arise in a vacuum due the uncertainty principle; Feynman diagrams use virtual particles to illustrate how properties are exchanged between real particles.

white dwarf   The collapsed remnant of a once-functioning star with a mass below the Chandrasekhar limit of 1.4 solar masses; remnant stars with masses above the limit collapse further to become neutron stars or black holes.

Bibliography

The Abraham Zelmanov Journal. "Biography of Karl Schwarzschild." Available online. URL: http://zelmanov.ptep-online.com/papers/zj-2008-b3.pdf

Aczel, Amir. *God's Equation: Einstein, Relativity, and the Expanding Universe.* New York: Basic Books, 1999.

American Institute of Physics. "Triumph of the Copenhagen Interpretation." Available online. URL: http://www.aip.org/history/heisenberg/p09.htm. Accessed February 15, 2011.

American Museum of Natural History. "John Michell and Black Holes." Available online. URL: http://www.amnh.org/education/resources/rfl/web/essaybooks/cosmic/cs_michell.html. Accessed February 15, 2011.

Asimov, Isaac. *How Did We Find Out About the Speed of Light?* New York: Walker Co., 1986.

Borowski, E.J. and J.M. Borwein. *The HarperCollins Dictionary of Mathematics.* New York: HarperCollins, 1991.

Boston University. "Mathematicians and other Oddities of Nature." Available online. URL: http://math.bu.edu/people/jeffs/mathematicians.html. Accessed February 15, 2011.

Casti, John L. *The One True Platonic Heaven.* Washington, D.C.: Joseph Henry Press, 2003.

Coles, Peter. "Einstein, Eddington, and 1919 Eclipse." Available online. URL: http://arxiv.org/abs/astro-ph/0102462. Accessed February 15, 2011.

Cox, Brian and Jeff Forshaw. *Why Does E = mc²?* Cambridge, Mass.: Da Capo Press, 2009.

Cromie, William J. "Physicists Slow Speed of Light." *The Harvard University Gazette.* Available online. URL: http://www.hno.harvard.edu/gazette/1999/02.18/light.html. Accessed February 15, 2011.

Dibner, Bern. *Oersted and the Discovery of Electromagnetism.* New York: Blaisdell Publishing Company, 1962.

Durant, Will and Ariel. *The Story of Civilization, vol. VIII: The Age of Louis XIV.* New York: Simon and Schuster, 1963.

Einstein, Albert. *Relativity: The Special and General Theory.* New York: Plume, 2006.

Ferguson, Kitty. *Tycho & Kepler: The Unlikely Partnership That Forever Changed Our Understanding of the Heavens.* New York: Walker & Company, 2002.

Ferris, Timothy. *Coming of Age in the Milky Way.* New York: William Morrow, 1988.

Ferris, Timothy. *The Whole Shebang: A State-of-the Universe(s) Report.* New York: Simon & Schuster, 1997.

Fowler, Michael. "Conserving Momentum: The Relativistic Mass Increase." Available on line. URL: http://galileoandeinstein.physics.virginia.edu/lectures/mass_increase.html. Accessed on July 11, 2011.

Fowler, Michael. "More Relativity: The Train and the Twins." Available online. URL: http://galileoandeinstein.physics.virginia.edu/lectures/sreltwins.html. Accessed February 15, 2011.

Frisch, David H. and James H. Smith. "Measurement of the Relativistic Time Dilation Using μ-Mesons." *Am. J. Phys.* 31 (1963): 342–355.

Galilei, Galileo. *Dialogue Concerning the Two Chief World Systems.* New York: The Modern Library, 2001.

Gardner, Martin. *Relativity Simply Explained.* Mineola, N.Y.: Dover, 1997.

Gates, Evalyn. *Einstein's Telescope: The Hunt for Dark Matter and Dark Energy in the Universe.* New York: W.W. Norton, 2009.

Georgia State University. "Einstein Velocity Addition." Available online. URL: http://hyperphysics.phy-astr.gsu.edu/hbase/relativ/einvel2.html. Accessed February 15, 2011.

Georgia State University. "Index of Refraction." Available online. URL: http://hyperphysics.phy-astr.gsu.edu/Hbase/geoopt/refr.html#c2. Accessed February 15, 2011.

Georgia State University. "Lorentz Transformation." Available online. URL: http://hyperphysics.phy-astr.gsu.edu/HBASE/relativ/ltrans.html. Accessed February 15, 2011.

Gibbs, Phil and Sugihara Hiroshi. "What is Occam's Razor?" Available online. URL: http://math.ucr.edu/home/baez/physics/General/occam.html. Accessed February 15, 2011.

Guéron, Eduardo. "Adventures in Curved Spacetime." *Scientific American* 301 (August 2009): 38–45.

Hawking, Stephen W. *A Brief History of Time: From the Big Bang to Black Holes*. New York: Bantam Books, 1988.

Hertzsprung, Ejnar. "Karl Schwarzschild." *The Astrophysical Journal* XLV (1917) 283-292.

Hirshfeld, Alan. *The Electric Life of Michael Faraday*. New York: Walker and Co., 2006.

Isaacson, Walter. *Einstein: His Life and Universe*. New York: Simon and Schuster, 2007.

Johnson, George. *The Ten Most Beautiful Experiments*. New York: Alfred A. Knopf, 2008.

Mahon, Basil. *The Man Who Changed Everything: The Life of James Clerk Maxwell*. Hoboken, N.J.: John Wiley and Sons, 2003.

Manning, Phillip. *Atoms, Molecules, and Compounds*. New York: Chelsea House, 2007.

Manning, Phillip. *Chemical Bonds*. New York: Chelsea House, 2009.

Manning, Phillip. *Gravity*. New York: Chelsea House, 2011.

Margenau, Henry and George Moseley Murphy. *The Mathematics of Physics and Chemistry*, 2nd ed. Princeton, N.J.: D. Van Nostrand, 1956.

Masters of Cinema. "22.XII.15 Verehrter Herr Einstein," translated to "Dear Mr. Einstein." Available online. URL: http://www.mastersofcinema.org/jan/tt.pdf. Accessed February 15, 2011.

Newton, Isaac. *Opticks*. New York: Dover Publications, 1952.

Newton, Isaac. *The Principia: Mathematical Principles of Natural Philosophy*, translated by I. Bernard Cohen and Anne Whitman. Berkeley: University of California Press, 1999.

Overbye, Dennis. *Einstein in Love: A Scientific Romance*. New York: Viking Penguin, 2000.

Pais, Abraham. *Subtle Is the Lord . . .* Oxford, U.K.: Oxford University Press, 1982.

Prosper, Harrison B. "Introduction to General Relativity." Available online. URL: http://www.physics.fsu.edu/Courses/Spring98/AST3033/Relativity/GeneralRelativity.htm. Accessed February 15, 2011.

Rosser, W.G.V. *Introductory Special Relativity*. London: Taylor & Francis, 1991.

Schombert, James. "Birth and Death of Stars." University of Oregon. Available online. URL: http://abyss.uoregon.edu/~js/ast123/lectures/lec05.html. Accessed February 15, 2011.

Scientific American. "Virtual Particles." Available online. URL: http://www. scientificamerican.com/article.cfm?id=are-virtual-particles-rea. Accessed February 15, 2011.

Stanford Encyclopedia of Philosophy. "William of Ockham." Available on line. URL: http://plato.stanford.edu/entries/ockham/. Accessed February 15, 2011.

University of South Wales. "The twin paradox: Is the symmetry of time dilation paradoxical?" Available online. URL: http://www.phys.unsw.edu. au/einsteinlight/jw/module4_twin_paradox.htm. Accessed February 15, 2011.

Wolfson, Richard. *Simply Einstein: Relativity Demystified.* New York: W.W. Norton, 2003.

Further Resources

Bais, Sander. *Very Special Relativity: An Illustrated Guide*. Cambridge, Mass.: Harvard University Press, 2007.

Casti, John L. *The One True Platonic Heaven*. Washington, D.C.: Joseph Henry Press, 2003.

Crease, Robert P. *The Great Equations: Breakthroughs in Science from Pythagorus to Heisenberg*. New York: W.W. Norton, 2008.

Fleisch, Daniel. *A Student's Guide to Maxwell's Equations*. New York: Cambridge University Press, 2008.

Gerach, Robert. *General Relativity from A to B*. Chicago: University of Chicago Press, 1981.

Marschall, Laurence A. *The Supernova Story*. Princeton, N.J.: Princeton University Press, 1988.

Stachel, John, ed. *Einstein's Miraculous Year: Five Papers That Changed the Face of Physics*. Princeton, N.J.: Princeton University Press, 1998.

Web Sites

History Channel's "The Universe: Light Speed"
http://www.youtube.com/view_play_list?p=44D9DE16B7E965FFA

This is a well-done, four-part series that explores the speed of light, how to slow it down to almost a standstill, and the efforts aimed at exceeding it.

Mysteries of Deep Space: Black Holes
http://www.youtube.com/watch?v=rw5trKz_kdc&feature=related

This site provides an image-rich exploration of black holes, especially the super-massive ones found in the centers of galaxies.

Nova's "Time Travel"

http://www.pbs.org/wgbh/nova/time/

> *Listen to Carl Sagan and other scientists discuss the possibilities of traveling through time.*

On the Electrodynamics of Moving Bodies

http://www.fourmilab.ch/etexts/einstein/specrel/www/

> *This is an English translation of Einstein's original paper on relativity published on June 30, 1905. Although a complete reading of it is beyond most students, it is worth perusing to get a feel for how Einstein developed the concept of special relativity.*

The Twin Paradox

http://math.ucr.edu/home/baez/physics/Relativity/SR/TwinParadox/twin_paradox.html

> *This site examines the famous paradox from several different viewpoints.*

University of Southampton's Institute of Sound and Vibration Research

http://www.isvr.soton.ac.uk/SPCG/Tutorial/Tutorial/Tutorial_files/Web-further-light.htm

> *This site has a good applet demonstrating the propagation of an electromagnetic wave and comparing it to a sound wave.*

What Is a Four-dimensional Space Like?

http://www.pitt.edu/~jdnorton/teaching/HPS_0410/chapters/four_dimensions/index.html

> *This Web site aims to help the viewer visualize a four-dimensional space. It is impossible for most (maybe all) of us to do this, but this site can help.*

Picture Credits

Index

About the Author

Phillip Manning is the author of eight previous books and approximately 200 magazine and newspaper articles. Two of his books— *Atoms, Molecules, and Compounds* and *Chemical Bonds*—were published as part of Chelsea House's ESSENTIAL CHEMISTRY series. Two others, *Gravity* and *Quantum Theory*, are part of the publisher's SCIENCE FOUNDATIONS series. Another book, *Islands of Hope*, won a National Outdoor Book award for nature and the environment. Manning has a Ph.D. in physical chemistry from the University of North Carolina at Chapel Hill. His Web site www.scibooks.org lists new books and book reviews about science.

Manning notes: "Jesse Miner read and commented on parts of the manuscript. Miner, who just completed his Ph.D. in astrophysics at the University of North Carolina at Chapel Hill, caught several errors. Regrettably, any that remain are entirely mine."